PRAISE FOR THE JESUS MASTER SERIES

Doc:

I applaud your JESUS MASTER series of books. Thanks for the chance to review them and give you my input.

I recommend them to anyone who wants to be at the top, and stay at the top, with their personal performance, attitude enhancement, business success, wealth enrichment, and family and spiritual growth.

For decades, I told my readers and audiences that motivation simply means moving yourself and moving others forward in the successful pursuit of better attitudes and better performance. The best way to do that, I told them, is to follow the teachings and walk in the footsteps of the master motivator, Jesus Christ.

That's the secret of life AT THE TOP.

See you at the top,
Zig Ziglar

My good friend Dr. Gallagher's new book, *JESUS CHRIST, MONEY MASTER*, is required reading for anyone who is looking for a highly practical and thoroughly biblical guide to financial success. Dr. Gallagher's financial expertise, coupled with his devotion to Jesus Christ, makes him the perfect person to write such a book. Dr. Gallagher reminds us that when we follow God's instructions for money management, we can experience His blessings NOW! In these times of economic chaos, he has provided us with sound wisdom for handling our money, based on the words of the wisest man who ever walked the earth. I highly recommend this book!

Dr. Robert Jeffress
Senior Pastor
First Baptist Church, Dallas

Jesus CHRIST

Money MASTER

Jesus CHRIST *Money* MASTER

The Wisest Words
Ever Spoken on Money

W. Neil Gallagher, PhD

BROWN
CHRISTIAN PRESS
A DIVISION OF
BROWN BOOKS PUBLISHING

Jesus Christ, Money Master
The Wisest Words Ever Spoken on Money

Brown Christian Press
16250 Knoll Trail Drive, Suite 205
Dallas, Texas 75248
www.BrownChristianPress.com
(972) 381-0009

A New Era in Publishing®

ISBN 978-1-61254-220-1
Library of Congress Control Number 2016930794

Printed in the United States
10 9 8 7 6 5 4 3 2 1

For more information or to contact the author, please go to
www.NeilGallagherBooks.com.

Dedicated to
S. Truett Cathy

. . . who by his lips and life dramatized the truth that the principles in *Jesus Christ, Money Master* deliver abundant profit, enduring enjoyment, and consistent progress for oneself and others.

Thank you, Truett.

Dr. Gallagher, S. Truett Cathy, and Scotty Gallagher in Truett Cathy's "treehouse."

The "Jesus Master" ® Series

Jesus has become as taboo as a four-letter word in our society, and Christians are often censored or attacked for their beliefs. This series is about putting the words and works of Jesus Christ back into the center of American culture, where they belong.

Again.

The five books in this series are not "faith-based," which is a politically correct euphemism to hide, or eliminate, one's biblical convictions. These five books are God-based, applying the teachings of Jesus to urgent and practical issues of contemporary culture . . . teachings that deliver profitable solutions leading to both eternal happiness and earthly success.

Jesus Christ, Money Master
Jesus Christ, Master Motivator
Jesus Christ, Master Teacher
Jesus Christ, Master Leader
Jesus Christ, Master Salesman

"Jesus Master" ® Series Registered Trademark, W. Neil Gallagher, PhD 2012

One Solitary Life[1]

Here is a man who was born in an obscure village, the child of a peasant woman. He grew up in another village. He worked in a carpenter shop until he was thirty. Then for three years he was an itinerant preacher.

He never owned a home. He never wrote a book. He never held an office. He never had a family. He never went to college. He never put his foot inside a big city. He never traveled two hundred miles from the place he was born. He never did one of the things that usually accompany greatness. He had no credentials but himself . . .

While still a young man, the tide of popular opinion turned against him. His friends ran away. One of them denied him. He was turned over to his enemies. He went through a mockery of a trial. He was nailed upon a cross between two thieves. While he was dying, his executioners gambled for the only piece of property he had on earth— his coat. When he was dead, he was laid in a borrowed grave through the pity of a friend.

Twenty long centuries have come and gone, and today he is a centerpiece of the human race and leader of the column of progress.

I am far within the mark when I say that all the armies that ever marched, all the navies that were ever built; all the parliaments that ever sat and all the kings that ever reigned, put together, have not affected the life of man upon this earth as powerfully as has that one solitary life.

Notes

1. James Allan Francis, *One Solitary Life*, 1–7. Published in the Congressional Record, December 23, 1969, vol. 115, p. 13105.

Contents

Introduction

Why He's Called Money Master

He's called a lot of things:

Son of God

Messiah

Lamb of God

The Anointed One

Son of Man

Teacher

Rabbi

The Lion of Judah

. . . and more.

But, Money Master?

Isn't this the guy (sorry, the God) who said, "It is harder for a rich man to enter heaven than for a camel to climb through the eye of a needle," "Happy are the poor in spirit for they shall see God," and "You cannot love God and money"?

Why call Jesus Christ the Money Master?

Because he mastered money and possessions in ways no one else has. Or can.

Donald Trump cannot command a fish to cough up cash.

Bill Gates cannot rip hunks of bread to feed five thousand.

Warren Buffett cannot speak water into wine.

Only the *owner* of New York's Trump Towers can make a fish cough up cash. Only the *owner* of food can rip hunks of bread to feed five thousand. Only the *owner* of wealth can speak water into wine.

Jesus was the wealthiest person. Ever! When you own the universe, you own it all: "Jesus described himself in one parable as the 'Husbandman' who had been sent to take care of the vineyard. He looked at the world and the people in it as his responsibility, his inheritance, and his heritage. The whole universe was his and he knew it."[1]

If the whole world is his, including our money, it just makes sense to look to the owner of all wealth for direction on how to use it. *Jesus Christ, Money Master* is a guide to a spiritual and financial journey that will enable you to answer one of life's most important questions:

What is my money for?

Here it is:

It's not your money.

God has a purpose for your life and your money. This is refreshing news because millions want to enjoy the truth that their money has meaning and purpose, transcending daily worries or fleeting pleasures. Spiritual truths and money strategies may strike you as unlikely bedfellows, but even "The Donald" himself recognizes the importance of acknowledging the creator of wealth when deciding how to use it. In his book *How to Think Like a Billionaire*, Donald Trump writes, "I'm sure some wise guy in the media is going to accuse me of comparing myself to God. I do not think I am God. I believe in God. If God ever wanted an apartment in the Trump Tower, I would immediately offer my best luxury suite at a very special price. I believe God is here, and I want decisions I make to reflect well on me when it's time for me to go to that big boardroom in the sky."[2]

Dave Ramsey, whom I've had the pleasure of having on my show several times, mixes spiritual truths with money strategies, and his books and seminars have helped countless people to overcome debt and embrace a liberating new lifestyle. In fact, if there were ever two guys who fulfilled Mordecai's statement to Esther, "You were sent into the kingdom for such a time as this," those guys are Dave Ramsey and Rick Warren, whose books and ministries have helped millions to discover the purpose that God has for their lives.

The point is that discovering the purpose of your money—like the purpose of your life as a whole—is necessarily a spiritual endeavor, even as your money and your life are inescapably entwined. Our decisions with money impact countless other aspects of our lives. We need direction in this critical area, and the perfect model to follow is

Jesus Christ, the greatest teacher of finances (and everything else) that has ever lived.

By his life and lips, Jesus dramatized four practical and powerful truths about money:

- Don't love it
- Do give it
- How to earn it
- How to make it grow

In *Jesus Christ, Money Master*, I document these four truths and show their relevance to contemporary opportunities with, and attacks on, your money. Jesus's teachings about money dramatize his brilliance as a money manager and propel him above anybody on Wall Street.

It's time to acknowledge this truth. It's time to give credit where credit is due:

- Jesus's Golden Rule, applied to Wall Street, would have prevented Bernie Madoff's churning of client accounts and Enron's "cooking the books."
- Jesus's ethical principles would have smashed deceptive practices of banks and brokerage firms exposed in Arthur Levitt's book *Take on the Street: What Wall Street and Corporate America Don't Want You to Know.*
- Jesus's "Tower Parable," showcasing the need for caution and the urgency of planning, would have protected millions of investors from their billions in losses in the market meltdowns of 2001, 2008, and the J. P. Morgan billion-dollar scandals of 2012.[3]

After reading this book, you will be able to apply the same principles that Jesus taught to your own life and your own money. Following Jesus's four truths will delight the buyer, worker, or investor—that's you—with profit, freedom, significance, and a sense of purpose. You can release the guilt and shame you carry from financial failures in your past, and you can embrace a future of forgiveness, hope, and opportunity. You will face financial decisions with confidence and security, knowing that the One who entrusted you with these resources will faithfully see you through as you earn, give, and grow your money with courage and integrity. Your money will no longer have a hold on your life or a claim on your happiness.

Follow the Master, and grab mastery over money.

Notes

1. Laurie Beth Jones, *Jesus, CEO* (New York: Hyperion Books, 1995) 35.
2. Donald J. Trump, *Trump: Think Like a Billionaire* (New York: Ballantine Books, 2004), xi.
3. Arthur Levitt, *Take On The Street: What Wall Street and Corporate America Don't Want You To Know* (Pantheon, 2002).

Divorce or Suicide

One Couple's Financial Crisis

"Dr. Gallagher, I came only because she said she's leaving for sure and taking the kids . . ." He locked his forearms on top of his Dallas Stars cap and rocked back and forth. "If this doesn't—"

She shot: "He was going to say *if* this doesn't work, and that's a big 'if.'" She stared at him, her chin jutting like a brick. "We came because he said he was out of here and was going to commit suicide. You see that bulge in his pocket? It's not money. He never has any. It's a gun. He said it's divorce, or suicide, or both."

Lester, age thirty-five, and wife Rachel, thirty-four, were seated in front of my desk.

"Tell me about it, Lester." I slipped my cell phone from my pocket, laid it atop my knee like balancing an egg, and scrolled to 911. "Deep breath, now. Relax. Tell me about it."

He leaned forward, pushing his knees against the desk. "For years, she runs up bills. Macy's, Sear's, Discover, you name it. Shoes? If they were combat boots, she could have outfitted an army."

"That's *not* the reason we're here!" She stood and pointed at him. "You and your toys, ski boots, jet doos, whatever, thousand-dollar barbeque grills, season tickets to the Stars. Gotta be the big spender, show all your buddies. Where are your buddies now, big guy, when we're fifty thousand in debt? They're calling me at work. Can't even keep up the co-payments on our health insurance, and the kids need shots, and Kevin's autism is not going to go away, and he needs that tutoring, and we can't even buy him or us the right food."

He slapped his hands on his knees and sprang up. "Why don't you ever cook, instead of having lunch with your girlfriends? Instead of ordering in pizza and Chinese food and barbeque, just stay home and cook."

"What's wrong with having lunch with friends?" She faced me squarely. "Gotta talk to somebody, Dr. Gallagher. I talk to friends who listen, but he stays after work to grab a beer or two. By the time he gets home, he's too woozy to talk."

"That's it." He stepped forward, an inch from her nose. "You never—"

I slammed my palms on the desk. "Stop. You saw the ground rules in the waiting room, and you agreed. We don't raise our voices. We don't use words like always and never. We report feelings, tough as it is, and we do not accuse. We focus on solutions."

I slid across the desk the sheets of ground rules that they had signed. "You don't want divorce. You don't want suicide. You don't want hate or accusations. That's why you came. That's why you signed the sheets. That's why you're here."

I waited a moment, letting the words sink in.

"Sit down, Lester," I whispered.

He sat.

"The reason for this meeting—let's cut to the chase—is that you're fifty thousand dollars in debt. You're both scared, and you're both mad. Is that right?"

"Yeah, I'm scared," Lester said, and stood again. "I'm mad at her, and I'm out of here."

"Lester, wait until you hear what Rachel has to say. Sit down, please," I whispered.

He sat.

"Rachel, you're scared and you're mad?"

"I'm not just scared for me. I'm scared for our kids." She cupped her hands to her eyes, and tears slid between her fingers. "What's going to happen to them? What if CPS comes in and says we can't manage our household budget? What if they say we're not fit parents? If we divorce, they'll be in court and hear the whole mess. And if he does commit suicide, that's easy for him. It's all over for us."

Lester stared at the floor. "Who's not the fit parent?"

"Lester," I said, "who are you mad at?"

"I'm mad at her, she runs up all those—"

"Wait. Wait. Think maybe you're mad at yourself for running up your debts? You say that you're both Christians, so in the Christian family, the man is the leader, the one responsible. Are you kind of mad at yourself for the mess your family is in?"

"I didn't get any help from her."

"I'm asking you, do you take *any* responsibility for the mess that you're in?"

"All right. Maybe I got a little bit carried away."

"Are you mad at yourself for allowing your family to get into the debt it's in?"

"That's part of it."

"Excellent, Lester. I'm proud of you. That's a good start." I looked at them both. "Let's look at a story that Jesus told about a guy that got mad at himself and got himself out of a mess. It's a story about a kid brother, a big brother, and a father who knew how to run."

I told them the story of the Prodigal Son. You know the story: A man has two sons, and the younger one asks for his share of the estate. No sooner has the father divided his property between them than the younger son heads off to a distant land and lives it up, burning through every last bit of his inheritance.

After he blows all his money on "wild living," a severe famine hits the whole country, and he finds himself so desperate for work and sustenance that he hires himself out to a local who sends him into the fields to feed pigs. The younger son is so hungry that he finds himself longing to eat the pods that he's giving to the pigs.

Then, a light bulb goes off, and he asks himself, "How many of my father's hired servants have food to spare, and here I am starving to death! I will go back to my father and say to him: 'Father, I have sinned against heaven and against you. I am no longer worthy to be called your son; make me like one of your hired servants.'"

He gets up, leaves behind his life with the pigs, and heads toward home. Here's how the story ends:

> But while he was still a long way off, his father saw him and was filled with compassion for him; he ran to his son, threw his arms around him and kissed him.
>
> The son said to him, "Father, I have sinned against heaven and against you. I am no longer worthy to be called your son."
>
> But the father said to his servants, "Quick! Bring the best robe and put it on him. Put a ring on his finger and sandals on his feet. Bring the fattened calf and kill it. Let's have a feast and celebrate. For this son of mine was dead and is alive again; he was lost and is found." So they began to celebrate.
>
> Meanwhile, the older son was in the field. When he came near the house, he heard music and dancing. So he called one of the servants and asked him what was going on. "Your brother has come," he replied, "and your father has killed the fattened calf because he has him back safe and sound."
>
> The older brother became angry and refused to go in. So his father went out and pleaded with him. But he answered his father, "Look! All these years I've been slaving for you and never disobeyed your orders. Yet you never gave me even a young goat so I could celebrate with my friends. But when this son of yours who has squandered your

property with prostitutes comes home, you kill the fattened calf for him!"

"My son," the father said, "you are always with me, and everything I have is yours. But we had to celebrate and be glad, because this brother of yours was dead and is alive again; he was lost and is found."

—Luke 15:11–32

I finished the story and faced Lester and Rachel. "What did the kid brother do? He took responsibility for the mess that he was in. That's number one. The Bible teaches that all of us have fallen flat on our faces, financial and otherwise. All, hey, beginning with me, Dr. G—all of us have made mistakes with many money decisions. Life is tough. No one's perfect. Join the club."

Everyone's Story / Everyone's Solution

We have all been financial flops at one time or another. We've all messed up when it comes to God's standards. Maybe it's with gossip, maybe adultery, or theft, lying, whatever. All of us have fallen flat on our faces, and this includes finances—ill-advised purchases, stupid financial decisions, bad jobs, impulsive spending.

As Paul wrote in Romans 3:10, there is none righteous, not even one. Lest anyone boast, we need a healthy dose of humility the next time we try to walk on water. We are far from perfect. If you're reading this and you're human, this includes you.

So what do we do with the resources we're given? With all the *negative* role models in view, how do we know which example to follow? There's a clear and *positive* answer: the Bible is the authority on life, and the Bible is the authority on money. That's why we call Jesus Christ the "Money Master."

For years I hosted a talk show, *The Money Doctor Show*, on a CBS flagship station in the DFW area, the nation's fourth largest market. Weekly, I answered questions about stocks, bonds, mutual funds, retirement planning, real estate, taxes, gold, insurance, annuities, trusts, wills, 401Ks, and other concerns. I knew then, as I know now, that wise decisions in these areas are only a piece of the puzzle. So I also talked about tithing, giving, saving, and stewardship as a normal part of a savvy and profitable money-management style.

And, when appropriate, I told a listener to pray about his or her financial decision. And I prayed with them, on the air.

It's not enough to be knowledgeable or educated about money matters. You have to turn to the One that the money belongs to in the first place.

Whether in my books, or speaking at Zig Ziglar's *Born to Win* conferences, or working individually with clients, or on television when CBS aired a documentary piece on Gallagher Financial, I stress that handling money is not an isolated aspect of your life; nor is it outside the scope of a daily walk with God. Far from it.

A robust retirement is the dream of many . . . is a good example. A robust retirement is financial, yes, but it is also physical, relational, emotional, and spiritual.

In my practice, we share with our clients—and follow ourselves—what we call "The Six P's." I share them with you as an example of how you, with the help of this book and an open heart toward the teachings of Christ concerning money, can accept responsibility for your past, take ownership of your present, and look eagerly toward the future.

The Six P's

Proclamation

You need a mission statement. Money, without purpose, is a wasted resource. My company's mission statement is right there in our lobby: "Our mission is to be a vehicle of God's profit, peace, comfort, and power to as many people as possible, helping first with their financial success and also with their spiritual, emotional, and family well-being." If you were to proclaim the purpose of your resources— financial and otherwise—what would it be?

Prayer

At the end of our motivational meeting each morning, we have a brief prayer. We thank God for living in America, we thank God for our clients, we pray for our clients, we pray for each other. It's voluntary and spontaneous. Many clients come in needing encouragement, whether the issue has to do with finances or not, and we set aside time to pray with them and counsel them. If you are seeking to turn around your financial ship, to fill the sails and steer a new course, then prayer is of the utmost importance.

Preservation of Capital

Protecting your wealth is not an ungodly thing to do. In fact, you can't utilize your assets to complete your mission if you haven't first preserved them. We'll talk about that more later.

Remember Warren Buffett's dictum: "Rule number one, keep the principal safe. Rule number two: remember rule number one!" It's time to shift your mind-set about money and to realize that savvy financial decisions are part of a fiscally sound (and spiritually sound) approach to money. Your principal and income should go only one way: up!

Preparation

Money and security are like oxygen and breathing. You never want to run out, and if you have an urgent concern, you need help right away. This is why I give my clients my cell number—I'm prepared to help them 24/7. When clients come in, we are prepared for their visit, and we have formulated plans that are uniquely suited for them. As you work through this book, you will not only take stock of your past and present, but you must prepare for the future that you wish to inhabit. Foresight and planning are key, as are learning from the principles taught by the greatest money master who ever lived (just a hint, it's not me). Success does not come from sheer, spontaneous serendipity; it requires preparation.

Professionalism

Whether you have a billion dollars or lack two nickels to rub together, one of your roles is that of a professional money manager, and professionalism means more than a well-tailored wardrobe and a knack for punctuality. It involves a constant reassessment of yourself and a willingness to change. As they say, when you're green, you're growing, and when you're ripe, you're rotten. Consider yourself green. This book will teach you strategies to increase your income, preserve your retirement, enrich your legacy planning, and improve your communication with others about money. More importantly, it will challenge you to examine your motives and your heart toward money—which can, sometimes uncomfortably, force us to examine our heart toward God.

Practice

Anyone can listen to advice, read a book, attend a seminar, or work through a study guide. The real test is whether you can put into practice what you have learned. Unless they are applied, the best principles, strategies, techniques, and surefire approaches to wisely earning, growing, and spending your money will add up to nothing when it comes to balancing that big checkbook in the sky. You must act on what you have learned. And learn from your mistakes. Utilize your resources intentionally, productively, compassionately, and soundly. Your mission statement is more than words. You practice what you preach.

Action is primary.

You've heard the story of the five frogs on a log. Four of them decide to jump. How many are left? Most people answer, "There's one left." Wrong. There are five left. Just because four decided to jump does not mean they followed through. Action is primary; action is urgent.

There are your six P's. They are each founded at their core on a truth I learned a long time ago: the Bible is the authority on life, and the Bible is the authority on money. Jesus is indeed the Money Master, and these are the reasons:

1. Jesus is the wealthiest person ever to walk on the face of the earth.
2. The reason we normally don't associate Jesus with "wealth" is because we associate "wealth" (in our own culture) with stocks, bonds, real estate, sports cars, net worth, jewelry, and other visible displays of financial power.
3. Jesus had no need of displays. As God, he owns the universe. He has the power of ownership over everything.
4. Because Jesus is the wealthiest person ever, he (uniquely) speaks with divine authority, compassion, and relevance concerning money.

Through my thirty years as a financial counselor, I have found beyond a shadow of a doubt that following the words and actions of Jesus Christ does, in fact, deliver:

Profitable choices

Productive work environments

Prudent investing

Debt liquidation

Tax control

Retirement security

Lifetime income

Business success

Family harmony

Doubt me? Then, do what the gospels say: "Come and see."

Laurie Beth Jones, in her book *Jesus, CEO*, wrote:

> Jesus did not consider himself a beggar king. He used his divine sense of ownership to create the goods he needed when he needed them. Jesus looked at the world and all the people in it as his responsibility, his inheritance, and his heritage. The whole universe was his, and he knew it. Perhaps that is one reason why the people called him king. It was the way he looked at the world and carried himself in it. "All that the Father has is mine," Jesus said. Every galaxy, every newborn sheep, every fish leaping into the net, all that the Father had was his, and he knew it. He owned it.[1]

He owns it all, including all the money in the world. When we practice his principles, we get the benefits, and he gets the glory.

Remember Lester and Rachel? They had hit bottom. They had fallen on their faces financially but also relationally, emotionally, and spiritually.

There in my office, I told them the story of the Prodigal Son, and afterward I asked Lester point blank: "Can you do what this guy did? Can you start by accepting responsibility for the choices you made?"

"Yes," he said. "I guess so."

"No guesses. Forget about Rachel. Forget about your buddies. You wrote checks; you used credit cards. Don't blame your parents or the credit card companies or Rachel. Do you take responsibility for your actions? Before you answer, I want to show you something."

I grabbed a yellow tablet and sketched a box with two spaces.

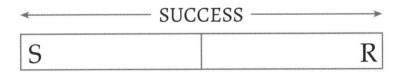

"On the far left is the letter S; on the far right is the letter R. There's a long space between them. That's how you spell success. S stands for stimulus and R stands for response. The stimulus is anything that we're hit with: temptations, fears, choices, whatever. Between the S and the R, there's this space, and in that space is God's gift called free will.

"Lester, when you are hit with the temptation, the stimulus, to buy grills, or guzzle up the family's food money, there's this space before you respond. That's what "responsible" means: *able to respond*. Do you accept the responsibility that maybe you didn't make the right choices before you responded? In other words, do you take responsibility for your actions in response to the temptations?"

"Yes."

"Excellent. Now do what the kid brother did. Forgive yourself. Will you do that?"

"Yes, I guess so. It was so dumb what I did. Yes."

"It gets better. In this story, the kid brother gets relief because he realizes that God forgives him. If he didn't believe that God would forgive him (remember, God and the Father are the same in the story), he would have stayed in that stinkin' mud or committed suicide. So off in the distance, he knew there was a God who forgave him and would give him another chance. So what did he do? He accepted responsibility for his financial flops, he forgave himself, he accepted God's forgiveness, and he took action. He got up and moved toward the running father."

I turned toward Rachel. Her face had softened as she listened in amazement to Lester's words. I said, "Rachel, it doesn't matter if this story is about a kid brother, or a husband, or a wife. Do you accept responsibility for your impulsive spending? Don't blame the credit card companies or your girlfriends or Lester. Do you accept responsibility for your spending?"

"Well, since Lester did, I guess—"

"No, no guesses. Do you accept responsibility for your impulsive spending?"

"Yes."

"Do you forgive yourself? Remember, when you did the impulsive spending, you were in the same category as me and Lester and millions of other people who have given in to greed or impulse or gluttony or envy or whatever. Do you forgive yourself?"

"Yes."

"Now do you accept God's forgiveness?"

"Yes. Yes. Yes."

"OK, now let's talk about actions. Remember, the kid brother got up and started walking toward the running father. Maybe he was running, too. Lester, here's the action for you. Turn on your chair, put your knees close to Rachel's knees, take her hands—good news, look; she's still got that ring on—look at her and say, 'Rachel, I forgive you.'"

He slowly turned in his chair, like there was glue underneath his thighs, and looked at Rachel. "I forgive you."

Tears slid down her cheeks. I snapped several Kleenex from a box on my desk. "Rachel, I'll dab your face. Keep holding Lester's hands. Look at him and say, 'I forgive you.'"

"I forgive you."

We spoke more about the story of the Prodigal Son, and I discussed the many lessons in the story—it's a tale of shame, failure, regret, repentance, broken relationships, repaired relationships, and envy. I wanted to look with them at the two financial flops in the story.

"The first one, of course, is the kid brother," I said. "What's his flop? *More*. That's what he wanted. More. The other financial flop is the big brother. Envy. You might say the kid brother's flop is 'I want more' and the big brother's flop is 'I want his.' Jesus shows us in many places where the attitude of the big brother leads. It leads to a heart filled with hate and resentment. Jesus not only showed us how

21

to turn a financial flop around, but he also taught us in the New Testament how to prevent these two attitudes."

The kid brother: "I want more." Solution: be content with what you have.

The big brother: "I want his." Solution: praise people who have done well. To praise another is a powerful preventative measure to resentment and envy.

"One more dynamic," I continued. "Some folks think that there was another flop, and that was the father. The father made a mistake by giving in to the kid brother's demands. No, the father knew this principle: If you love something, let it go. If it comes back, it's yours. If it doesn't come back, it wasn't yours to begin with.

"The father recognized the risk of parenthood: When your child is born, you rip your heart out of your body, and you give it to your child and say, 'Here. It's yours. Do with it whatever you want.' That's the gift of free will. That's the gift God gives us. We can train, encourage, discipline, and admonish, but at the end, it's free will. That's what the father recognized. That's what God recognizes, the gift of free will.

"God expects us to reciprocate with love and gratitude and service, and the kid brother finally got it. So did you two today. I am proud of you."

And I was.

No divorce, no suicide, no blaming, and we started building a financial future.

Jesus knows how to handle financial flops.

We are all financial flops at some point, and this brings pain and sorrow. But we have been given the gift of free will, which exists in that space between stimulus and response. You must choose how you will act and how you hold yourself accountable, which means (a) accepting responsibility for what brought the pain and sorrow and (b) embracing the pain and sorrow realistically. This is way different from placing the blame on others, and it's way different from denying there has been a tragedy or a reversal, financial or otherwise.

Accept pain and push forward. Stop the whining. Lester and Rachel did, and so did the kid brother in the story.

And so can you. It's never too late to make a decision to turn things around. The amazing gift of free will includes the opportunities to accept responsibility, forgiveness, and blessings, as well as the freedom to respond through loving thankfulness and generosity. Your money can lead to your downfall or contribute to your greatest legacy. You decide how *your* story will end. Much is left to be written, by you, in your story. The choice is yours.

Notes

1. Laurie Beth Jones, *Jesus, CEO* (New York: Hyperion Books, 1995), 4.

Jesus on Money

Don't Love It

When you love money, you'll never have enough.
You'll be infected by the disease called more.

—Billy Graham

It's not your money.

And you say, *"Like hell it isn't!* I worked hard, very hard for it! Don't give me that crap that it is God's money! It's *my* money—every blood and sweat dollar. I worked many jobs for it. I studied and trained for those jobs. I put up with jerks for years. I showed up for work for years—even when I did not feel like it. It's my money, and I'll do what I please with it!"

Really?

Who gave you the brains and body to acquire the skills to get the job? You earn your brains and body, too?

If you were born in America, who engineered your birth here, so you could work *where* you want, *when* you want, in a profession you wanted? You earn your birth, too? Perhaps you should have the attitude of Warren Buffett, the world's richest investor, who said, "My wealth has come from a combination of living in America, some lucky genes, and compound interest. Both my children and I won what I call the ovarian lottery. For starters, the odds against my birth taking place in the United States were at least thirty to one."

Do you have the grateful attitude of a Warren Buffet, or are you like the braggart flea lounging in the elephant's ear? The elephant clumped and stomped across the suspension bridge, forcing it to creek and sway. At the end of the elephant's loud march, the flea climbed to the top of the elephant's head and shouted, "Wow, we really made that bridge shake!"

People who scream, "My money!" are like the naive and arrogant flea. They earned it (or won it or inherited it), so they deserve it all! They also scream, "My money!" and clutch it like it's their rubber life raft of happiness, and then they panic when the air seeps out, when the money fades, and they start to drown.

Like lottery lady: "Dr. Gallagher, I have only $900,000 left."

Only $900,000? Left?! Hey, lady, if you don't want the $900,000, I know hundreds who could use it. These were the first thoughts racing through my mind.

She sat in the wingback burgundy chair in my office, on the other side of the coffee table blanketed with *Investment Review, Christianity Today, Prevention, Psychology Today,* and many others. Over the years, that chair had embraced many visitors, who gushed out a variety of problems and asked me for solutions:

- The widow with $1 million rotting in her non-interest checking account, earning nothing. (Too scared to do anything.) And . . . she was being charged a "management fee" by the bank!
- The retired school teachers, husband and wife, who wanted to roll over their $300,000 retirement plans. They did not have a clue as to whom they wanted as beneficiaries, nor did they have the simplest of estate documents. No will, no trust, no powers of attorney, no directive to physicians, no tax-saving strategies, no income-enhancement plan, and no legacy plans.
- The mother grieving over her seventeen-year-old runaway. She would do anything to get him back. She had no money and could hire no lawyers.
- The airline pilot who five years earlier had $650,000 at Big Brokerage firm. By the time he consulted with me, he had $45,000. His account had been churned by New York and St. Louis brokers. ("Dr. Gallagher, how am I going to make it the rest of my life? What do I do? Do I sue them? How am I going to get that money back? *How am I going to make it?*")
- The two Oklahoma Indian chiefs—what they called themselves and what their driver's licenses stated— who wanted me to transfer $10 million in gold into the US for them, alleging they had the protection of Indian lands and federal rights. (Thanks, but no thanks.)
- The daughter of the Mexican ambassador who had received a huge inheritance.
- And a thousand more.

The $900,000 lady in front of me had to be weirdest of all.

Maybe that's too strong. Most bizarre, maybe? Most pitiful? Most dramatic? This lady, like millions of others, was systematically ravaging her peace of mind through wild mismanagement of her personal and financial resources.

She continued: "I've been walking the streets and sleeping in my car. I was fooling around with the dial and heard you at the end of an interview. I heard you say there's always a solution. So I called and told the receptionist a little bit about what I needed, that I just needed to talk to somebody. I thought maybe you could see me in a couple of weeks. But she told me to come in now because I need help."

Her story: "My husband and I were two of the first winners of the Texas lottery, $35 million. Back then they were giving out lump sums, and after taxes it was $17 million. Well, my husband and I split up. We each got $8.5 million. I had a parade of people knocking on my door, sending me FedEx's, phone calls, telegrams, certified letters. Second and third cousins, classmates from the first grade, punks on the street . . . they were all after me. At first, I gave away a lot of the money just to get people off my back, and then I invested a lot of it real fast and real stupid. Oil wells, penny stocks, new restaurants, real estate that I never even looked at. I was spending money like I had $80 million rather than $8 million. I know now I've got to find a place where I can put the rest of this, where people will stop hounding me and I can pay my bills and my taxes without being wiped out, and I can have enough to live on in some privacy and some peace of mind the rest of my life."

She dragged out a shopping bag full of wrinkled and mud-smeared statements: mutual funds, insurance papers, stocks and bonds, banks, real estate, and more. I laid the statements flat on the coffee table, examining them one at a time, asking her questions about each to determine her suitability, investment profile, and future needs. I collected the usual information:

- Need for income
- Tolerance for risk
- Tax obligations
- Debt obligations
- Family obligations (anyone out there dependent upon you)
- Major repairs coming up
- Major medical expenses coming up, long-term care needs
- Estate protection: wills, trusts, liability protection, powers of attorney
- Legacy planning, beneficiary information

After reviewing this list I asked, "What do you want to do going forward with the money?"

"Nothing! I do not want to touch it. I want to leave it alone, except for a little income when I need it. How much can I take?"

She was afraid to take out one dollar for food or clothes or housing. She was paranoid about spending any money on anything. I assured her she had enough money to buy a change of clothes, get a good meal, and go to a hotel that night and get refreshed.

She took me up on my instructions.

She returned the next day, and we set up a plan for her to accomplish her goals of having safety, privacy, her bills paid, a guaranteed principal, and guaranteed life income. I assured her that by setting this up correctly, she would be free of predators and free of her own compulsive habits.

Hers was the standard lottery story . . . with one exception: hers had a happy ending.

If she followed my advice.

At this writing, she's still on track.

Hers is unlike most lottery stories, where the winners get tragically derailed and collapse into despair and destruction. This is because there are three approaches to money—love it, loathe it, or leverage it—and most lottery winners fall into the first camp. Sociologists who track the lifestyles of lottery winners tell us that:

- Shortly after winning the lottery, many lottery winners were *more miserable* than they were before they won their truckloads of money. And their destructive lifestyles showed it.
- This is because, fundamentally, they loved money and thought the money would bring them happiness.
- And, since money brings happiness, so they thought, they should spend a lot of it fast to get happy fast.

And other sad but true stories include:

1. Jack Whittaker had one of the biggest pots in US history, $113 million. Shortly after his torrid love affair with greed—after spending and spending and spending—he was sued for bouncing checks at several casinos. He was ordered by the court to undergo rehab after being arrested on drunken driving charges several times. His vehicle and business had been burglarized various times. He was sued by the father of an eighteen-year-old boy, a friend of his granddaughter's, who was found dead in Whittaker's house. Whittaker ended up besieged and broke.

2. Karen Cohen won $1 million in an Illinois lottery. Shortly after that, she filed for personal bankruptcy. A federal jury convicted her of lying to the bankruptcy court about her receipt of lottery checks, and she was sentenced to twenty-two months in federal prison.

3. Billy Bob Harrell won $31 million in the lottery. He committed suicide when the money ran out.

4. William "Bud" Post won $16.2 million in the Pennsylvania Lottery, only to have a brother try to kill him for the inheritance. Post spent all his winnings in a couple of years. He was living off social security at the time of his death.

5. Evelyn Adams won the New Jersey lottery twice in the mid-'80s for a total of $5.4 million. She gambled all her winnings. At last report, she was destitute and living in a trailer.

6. Suzanne Mullins won $4.2 million in a Virginia lottery, and shortly after that, she was sued for nonpayment of a loan. The judge ordered her to pay $154,147 in bad

debts. The lawyer pleaded with the court and provided evidence that she had no money left.

7. Shefik Talmadge won $6.7 million in the Arizona lottery in 1988. A few years later, after a string of bad investments, she declared bankruptcy.

8. Victoria Zeli shared an $11 million Powerball jackpot with her husband in the early 2000s. A few years later, the money was gone, and she was serving seven years in a Minnesota prison. She was finally convicted in a drug-and-alcohol-induced collision that killed one person and paralyzed another.

9. Gerald Muswagon was all smiles as his troubled life took a fairy-tale turn when he won a $10 million lottery jackpot. A short time after that, he hanged himself in his parents' garage.

10. Eric Wagner won the Illinois lottery jackpot. A year later, he was sentenced to thirty months in prison on gun and drug charges.

Deena Winter, in her article "Winning the Lottery Isn't Always a Dream," summarized this tragic pattern:

> It seemed as though financial planner Michael Begin was deliberately trying to rain on Mr. and Mrs. Lincoln's lottery parade when he and his partner, Darl LePage, sent out a Wednesday warning that Powerball winners' joy may be short-lived.
>
> "The reality is that most lottery winners will squander away their winnings in a few years," the Connecticut financial advisers said in a news release. "In the process, they will see family and

friendships destroyed and the financial security they hoped for disappear . . ."

"No one worries about the true impact on lives," Begin said. "Lottery winners just start spending. They spend it on toys, they spend it on luxuries, bad investments, scams. There are people coming out of the woodwork trying to take advantage of people. They become a huge target."

"Take a deep breath," says Begin. "The money is only a tool, not a magic cure. Seek out solid professional advice, and make sure your team of advisors works together closely, and that they focus on your family before they plan for your money."[1]

Worse yet, said the advisors who have served clients in eighteen states, winning a bunch of money doesn't build character; instead, it "reveals character and magnifies all the good and weak traits the winner lives by."

Indeed money does reveal character:

A man picked up a woman at a bar.

"Let's go to my apartment and have sex. I'll pay you $1,000."

"Let's go!"

On the way, he said, "Would you have sex with me for $500?"

"OK."

Getting closer to the apartment, he then asked, "Would you have sex with me for $100?"

"If it's a quickie."

Finally, "Would you have sex with me for $50?"

"What do you think I am, Mister?"

"We already know what you are. We're just haggling about the price."

It's because of this assault on character, self-esteem, and peace of mind that Jesus warned about the love of money:

> Truly I tell you, it is hard for someone who is rich to enter the kingdom of heaven. (Matt. 19:23)

> But woe to you who are rich, for you have already received your comfort. (Luke 6:24)

> This is how it will be with whoever stores up things for themselves but is not rich toward God. (Luke 12:21)

> When Jesus heard this, he said to him, "You still lack one thing. Sell everything you have and give to the poor, and you will have treasure in heaven. Then come, follow me." When he heard this, he became very sad, because he was very wealthy. (Luke 18:22–23)

The lottery winners, and other lovers of money, don't get it.

The truth is that money will buy . . .

> A bed but not sleep,
> Books but not brains,
> Food but not appetite,
> Finery but not beauty,
> A house but not a home,
> Medicine but not health,

> Luxuries but not love,
> Amusements but not happiness,
> Religion but not salvation,
> A good life but not eternal life,
> A passport to everywhere except
> contentment now and heaven later.

When people love money, they miss contentment and get hooked on two big drugs called greed and selfishness.

They spend money they don't have, for things they don't need, to impress people they don't like. They sink into a pit of despair where their outgo exceeds their income, and their upkeep becomes their downfall.

Here is the story of one man's downfall:

> There was a rich man who was dressed in purple and fine linen and lived in luxury every day. At his gate was laid a beggar named Lazarus, covered with sores and longing to eat what fell from the rich man's table. Even the dogs came and licked his sores.
>
> The time came when the beggar died and the angels carried him to Abraham's side. The rich man also died and was buried. In Hades, where he was in torment, he looked up and saw Abraham far away, with Lazarus by his side. So he called to him, "Father Abraham, have pity on me and send Lazarus to dip the tip of his finger in water and cool my tongue, because I am in agony in this fire."
>
> But Abraham replied, "Son, remember that in your lifetime you received your good things, while

Lazarus received bad things, but now he is comforted here and you are in agony. And besides all this, between us and you a great chasm has been set in place, so that those who want to go from here to you cannot, nor can anyone cross over from there to us."

He answered, "Then I beg you, father, send Lazarus to my family, for I have five brothers. Let him warn them, so that they will not also come to this place of torment."

Abraham replied, "They have Moses and the Prophets; let them listen to them."

"No, father Abraham," he said, "but if someone from the dead goes to them, they will repent."

He said to him, "If they do not listen to Moses and the Prophets, they will not be convinced even if someone rises from the dead."

—Luke 16:19–31

Please note: The rich man in this story was not in hell because he had money; nor was Lazarus in heaven because he had none. It was the attitude about money, God, and others that was critical and life changing.

Correction: Not *life* changing, but *eternity* changing.

Heaven is a place of God's love, pure love, agape love . . . love for others.

Loving God and loving others cannot exist in the same place as selfishness or love of self. Loving self is dramatized in one's love of money. Love of God and love of money cannot occupy the same space any more than sunshine and nighttime can occupy the same space. One drives out the other.

The rich man in the story was a man who was:

- For me,
- For me,
- For me.

This is what hell is. Hell is a place chosen by people who lived a lifestyle of love of *me, me, me* and a love of *money, money, money*. Hell is for people who throughout their lives ignored God and ignored service to others . . . the same way the rich man ignored the needs of Lazarus. For the rich man, and his contemporaries, it's not that God and others are second. It is that God and others do not exist.

That's what the rich man was and continues to be: me first! It does not matter whether you have a few billion or a few bucks. It's me first and none for you. That's hell on earth, and that's hell in eternity. Yes, hell is a real place where people suffer torment for their choices in denying God and denying service to others, dramatized in their choices about money.

Jesus's perspective on this attitude was magnified in Revelation: "You say, 'I am rich; I have acquired wealth and do not need a thing.' But you do not realize that you are wretched, pitiful, poor, blind, and naked." (Rev. 3:17)

The rich man's attitude was "I don't need God, I don't need you, and I certainly don't need to help people." In the Luke 15 passage, the rich man, absorbed in his own possessions, ignored the poor man Lazarus.

Jesus left the riches of heaven to fill a human body, to serve men and women. Serving God and mankind is heaven on earth and heaven later. Serving only oneself is hell on earth and hell later. The people who live only to serve themselves deny themselves the divine riches of heavenly joy now and heavenly joy later.

Because of his concern for us and our heaven-on-earth happiness, God through his Holy Spirit issued several warnings expanding Jesus's teachings:

> A leader must not be given to darkness, nor be violent, but gentle. Not quarrelsome, and not a lover of money. (1 Tim. 3:3)

> People will be lovers of themselves, lovers of money, boastful, proud, abusive, disobedient to their parents, ungrateful, unholy . . . (2 Tim. 3:2)

> Keep your lives free from the love of money and be content with what you have, because God has said, "Never will I leave you: Never will I forsake you." (Heb. 13:5)

> For the love of money is the root of all kinds of evil. Some people, eager for money, have wandered from the faith and pierced themselves with many griefs. (1 Tim. 6:10)

So . . . *Why* is the love of money the root of all evil? Because when people love money, they discover . . .

Money Never Satisfies

Money by itself does not make one happy. People in love with money are always after more; enough is never enough. They end up like dead monkeys.

Primitive hunters in Africa build a box to trap monkeys. At the bottom of the box, they put a fragrant banana, and the box has a hole just large enough for a monkey to push his hand through, provided his palm is open and fingers are extended. After he grabs the banana with his fingers wrapped around it, he now has a large fist, so large it won't fit back through the hole. He yanks and he pulls, but he is a victim of his own cage of greed. He continues to yank and pull until the creative hunter shows up, bangs him over the head, and has monkey meat for dinner.

Greed robs people of the riches of real freedom and the joys of enduring happiness.

The article "Would You Be Happier If You Were Richer? A Focusing Illusion" puts it this way:

> Surveys in many countries conducted over decades indicate that, on average, reported global judgments of life satisfaction or happiness have not changed much over the last four decades, in spite of large increases in real income per capita. While reported life satisfaction and household income are positively correlated in a cross-section of people at a given time, increases in income have been found to have mainly a transitory effect on individuals' reported life satisfaction.[2]

At best, the accumulation of money provides a fleeting and *temporary* high, a "transitory effect."

Love of Money Brings Out the Worst in Us

When people love money, they steal. Because, in their minds, enough is never enough. They steal to get more. They're always afraid someone is going to steal from them.

They lie. And then they lie and lie and lie again. Like my wise mother told me, "Tell one lie, and you've got to tell others."

They cheat, justifying their cheating on the claim that someone is always cheating them.

Screw them before they screw you.

Eat or be eaten.

Love of Money Destroys Us

When people love money, they live in fear, knowing that their lying, cheating, and stealing will one day catch up to them. Again, as my wise mother said, "There are always two people who know: God knows, and you know."

They collect it too fast. Getting rich quick . . . it's like eating a steak too quickly. Chunks of meat can stick in your windpipe and choke you.

When people love money, the attitude of envy eats their stomachs. They are outraged and depressed by seeing people who have more money than they do.

In *Neighbors as Negatives: Relative Earnings and Well-Being*, Professor Erzo F. P. Luttmer writes:

I agree with John Stuart Mill's observation that men do not desire to be rich, but richer than other men. Of course, the belief that people compare themselves with others around them goes back much further. After all, the framer of the Ten Commandments apparently judged it necessary to forbid humans from coveting their neighbors' possessions. Not all humans, however, appear to abide by this commandment . . .[3]

No Cost Is Too High

When people love money, they'll do anything to get it, including selling their souls. You remember the scene in Stephen Vincent Benet's classic "The Devil and Daniel Webster":

> It was about the last straw for Jabez Stone. "I vow," he said, and he looked around him kind of desperate. "I vow it's enough to make a man want to sell his soul to the devil, just so's he can get ahead."
>
> . . . Notice is always taken sooner or later, just like the Good Book says, and sure enough, next day about suppertime, a dark-dressed stranger drove up in a handsome buggy and asked for Jabez Stone.
>
> Jabez knew who it was. He didn't like the looks of the stranger, nor the way he smiled with his teeth . . .
>
> But having passed his word, more or less, Jabez stuck to it, and they went out behind the barn and

made their bargain. Jabez Stone had to prick his finger to sign, and the stranger lent him a silver pen. The wound healed clean, but it left a little white scar.[4]

Later in the story, had it not been for the oratorical skill of Daniel Webster in front of a "jury from hell," the exchange of soul for money would have been fulfilled and Jabez Stone would have been doomed.

Bounties of Blessings Are Missed

People who love money deny themselves the riches of gratitude. They are so obsessed with getting, getting, getting that they ignore the power and pleasure of being *grateful* for what they have.

Tragically, they never enjoy the following truths. Grateful people:

- Are more optimistic
- Exercise more
- Think more creatively
- Bounce back from adversity faster
- Are less intimidated by challenges
- Have higher immune response
- Are more alert and interested
- Are more adventurous
- Live longer
- Are more likely to help others
- Are more likable
- Are more tolerant

- Are better employees, managers, students, teachers, or team leaders
- Do better on tests
- Are less bored
- Are more hopeful
- Are more humble

Gratitude is the opposite of greed. Greed is inward-directed, eating at a person's sense of well-being and filling that person with pessimism as the greed metastasizes in the belly.

Gratitude is like love and forgiveness: it is an outward-directed emotion and action. Gratitude provides relief and joy to the one who feels it and expresses it, and to those who are the happy recipients of it.

Jesus directly identified the dangers of loving money in three statements:

- *Selfishly satisfied*
  "But woe to you who are rich, for you have already received your comfort" (Luke 6:24).

- *Reluctant to leave riches*
  "When Jesus heard this, he said to him, 'You still lack one thing. Sell everything you have and give to the poor, and you will have treasure in heaven. Then come, follow me.'

  "When he heard this, he became very sad, because he was very wealthy. Jesus looked at him and said, 'How hard it is for the rich to enter the kingdom of God! Indeed, it is easier for a camel to go through the eye of a needle than for someone who is rich to enter the kingdom of God'" (Luke 18:22–25).

- *Deceitful*

  "The seed falling among the thorns refers to someone who hears the word, but the worries of this life and the deceitfulness of wealth choke the word, making it unfruitful" (Matt. 13:22).

  For all the dangers associated with greed listed above, Jesus warns us *not* to love money.

The cure for loving money, for some, is to loathe it. Is it like the old King James description: Money is "filthy lucre"?

No, we need not loathe money. Loathing money is as stupid, unscriptural, and unproductive as loving it. Loathing money is the extreme opposite of loving it, and its danger is showcased in this story of a London beggar, attributed to Olehile Fischer Thataone:

> An old man lived in a certain part of London and he would wake up every morning and go to the subway. He would get the train right to Central London, and then sit at the street corner and beg. He would do this every single day of his life. He sat at the same street corner and begged for almost twenty years.
>
> His house was filthy, and a stench came out of the house and it smelled horribly. The neighbors could not stand the smell anymore, so they

summoned the police officers to clear the place. The officers knocked down the door and cleaned the house. There were small bags of money all over the house that he had collected over the years.

The police counted the money, and they soon realized that the old man was a millionaire. They waited outside his house in anticipation to share the good news with him. When he arrived home that evening, he was met by one of the officers who told him that there was no need for him to beg anymore as he was a rich man now, a millionaire.

He said he didn't care for the money and could find no use for it. Then he went into his house and locked the door. The next morning he woke up as usual, went to the subway, got into the train, and sat at the street corner and continued to beg.

The people who got caught up in the Children of God camps back in the '60s and '70s also had an unhealthy relationship with money. I visited one deep in the deserts of West Texas. Men and women, girls and boys, were wearing burlap robes tied with frayed ropes. I admired their sincerity and devotion, but I was grieved with their warped attitude toward money.

They loathed it.

Ostensibly self-sufficient, they raised their own chickens, vegetables, and fruits. On weekends, they piled into old VW buses and went to campuses around the country with signs: "Repent." "The kingdom of God is near." "Jesus hates sin." "Decadence destroys you." "Live pure." "Retreat from the world." "Money is evil."

While they were very nice and gave me and my companions a tour, in my opinion, the basis for their lifestyle was a misapplication of the scriptures that say, "If you love me, you will sell all your possessions and follow me," "A man who does not hate his mother and father cannot follow me," and similar passages.

In my view, we are to be *in* the world but not *of* the world. How do we penetrate and redeem culture if we stand outside of it? Being in the world requires a proper respect and use for money.

There is a balance between loving it and loathing it. Leverage it, Jesus teaches.

It seems to be a bizarre example, at first glance, but one of the stories that Jesus told illustrating the necessity of leveraging money, time, and opportunity is in Luke 16, the parable of the *unjust* steward:

> Jesus told his disciples: There was a rich man whose manager was accused of wasting his possessions. So he called him in and asked him, "What is this I hear about you? Give an account of your management, because you cannot be manager any longer."
>
> The manager said to himself, "What shall I do now? My master is taking away my job. I'm not

strong enough to dig, and I'm ashamed to beg—I know what I'll do so that, when I lose my job here, people will welcome me into their houses."

So he called in each one of his master's debtors. He asked the first, "How much do you owe my master?"

"Nine hundred gallons of olive oil," he replied.

The manager told him, "Take your bill, sit down quickly, and make it four hundred and fifty."

Then he asked the second, "And how much do you owe?"

"A thousand bushels of wheat," he replied.

He told him, "Take your bill and make it eight hundred."

The master commended the dishonest manager because he had acted shrewdly. For the people of this world are more shrewd in dealing with their own kind than are the people of the light. I tell you, use worldly wealth to gain friends for yourselves, so that when it is gone, you will be welcomed into eternal dwellings.

Whoever can be trusted with very little can also be trusted with much, and whoever is dishonest with very little will also be dishonest with much. So if you have not been trustworthy in handling worldly wealth, who will trust you with true riches? And if you have not been trustworthy with someone else's property, who will give you property of your own? (Luke 16:1–12)

We can argue about motive, timing, and propriety, but the fact is that Jesus praised the man who was "trustworthy in handling worldly wealth." Paraphrasing: "Show me you can leverage money a little, and I'll let you leverage a lot."

A contemporary example of leveraging money is the story told by Russ Conwell[5] in his magnificent book *Acres of Diamonds*:

> I say that you ought to get rich, and it is your duty to get rich. How many of my pious brethren say to me, "Do you, a Christian minister, spend your time going up and down the country advising young people to get rich, to get money?" Yes, of course I do.
>
> They say, "Isn't that awful! Why don't you preach the gospel instead of preaching about man's making money?" Because to make money honestly is to preach the gospel. That is the reason. The men who get rich may be the most honest men you find in the community.
>
> "Oh," but says some young man here tonight, "I have been told all my life that if a person has money he is very dishonest and dishonorable and mean and contemptible." My friend, that is the reason you have none, because you have that idea of people. The foundation of your faith is altogether false . . .
>
> Says another young man, "I hear sometimes of men who get millions of dollars dishonestly." Yes, of course you do, and so do I. But they are so

rare a thing in fact that the newspapers talk about them all the time as a matter of news until you get the idea that all the other rich men got rich dishonestly . . .

We preach against covetousness, and you know we do, in the pulpit . . . and use the terms about "filthy lucre" so extremely that Christians get the idea that when we stand in the pulpit we believe it is wicked for any man to have money . . .

Money is power, and you ought to be reasonably ambitious to have it! You ought because you can do more good with it than you can without it. Money printed your Bibles, money builds your churches, money sends your missionaries, and money pays your preachers . . . I say, then, you ought to have money. If you can honestly attain unto riches . . . it is our Christian and godly duty to do so. It is an awful mistake of these pious people to think you must be awfully poor in order to be pious.[6]

Money:

Love it,
Loathe it,
or
Leverage it.

When you leverage money as the Scriptures teach, you acknowledge that it is all God's to begin with. As a good steward, you will search for opportunities to give, earn, and grow the money he has entrusted to you.

In this sense, all the points and principles that follow in this book tie back to this initial decision to leverage the resources God has granted—and the realization that your money, like your life, has a greater purpose. With this book, you grab your money and enjoy your purpose.

Congratulations.

Notes

1. Deena Winters, "Financial Planners: Winning the Lottery Isn't Always a Dream," *Lincoln Journal Star*, February 26, 2006.
2. Daniel Kahneman, et. al., "Would You be Happier if You Were Richer? A Focusing Illusion," *Science*, 312: 1908–1910.
3. Erzo F. P. Luttmer, "Neighbors as Negatives: Relative Earnings and Well-Being," *The Quarterly Journal of Economics* (August 2005): 963.
4. Stephen Vincent Benét, *The Devil and Daniel Webster and Other Writings* (New York: Penguin Books), 16.
5. Conwell was a lawyer and Baptist minister. He was founder and the first president of Temple University. He also founded Conwell's School of Theology, which later became Gordon Conwell Theological Seminary, one of the largest interdenominational seminaries in the United States. The entire speech, "Acres of Diamonds" (from which this is excerpted), was delivered live by Conwell over six thousand times.
6. Russell Herman Conwell, *Acres of Diamonds*. (New York: Harper & Brothers, 1915).

2

Jesus on Money

2a. Don't Love It

2b. Do Give It

→ *Part One: The Gift of Giving*

Part Two: Are You a Flint, Sponge, or Honeycomb?

2c. How to Earn It

Part One: Employee

Part Two: Self-Employed

Part Three: Business Leader: The Boss

2d. How to Make It Grow: Power, Profit, Peace of Mind, and Putting People First

Part One: Jesus on Growing Money

Part Two: Jesus's Talent Parable

Part Three: Jesus's Tower Parable

Part Four: The Tower Parable and the Power of Critical Reasoning

Part Five: Jesus's Mustard Seed Parable: Let My Money Grow

Part Six: Jesus on Taxes

Do Give It

The Gift of Giving

The reason to make money is to give it away.

—Donald Trump
How to Think Like a Billionaire

Give, and it will be given to you. A good measure, pressed down, shaken together and running over, will be poured into your lap. For with the measure you use, it will be measured to you.

—Luke 6:38

The Gift of Giving

From Dallas, go west on I-20 a hundred miles and you come to the town of Ranger. You'll see a billboard on I-20 reading: "RANGER, TEXAS, THE OIL BOOM THAT WON THE WAR."

They're talking about World War I.

In the early 1900s, a legendary oil boom put Texas on the global map along with its extravagant tales of ocean-sized ranches and Pecos Bill legends. A tiny Bible church in Ranger discovered they had a gusher on their property.

Instantly endowed.

Instantly wealthy.

It's Wednesday night, and the deacons are meeting. They are planning Sunday's service, and a young guy quips, "Well, we can eliminate tithes and offering. We don't need an offering anymore." He chuckles. "We've got about $3,500 *a month* comin' up from those royalties!"

(LOTS of money back then.)

Brother Ledbetter, a wise old deacon, chides, "No, we'll still have an offering comin' up this Sunday and every Sunday. We'll still ask people to give to help support the preacher, to help with education, Bible classes, missions, for benevolence, all the things we do. Sure enough, we'll still have an offering. We're going to give because *we need to give.*

"Giving is God's gift to us," he continues. "If we don't give, we'll dry up and die."

High five to Brother Ledbetter! The gift of giving *is* the gift of *life.*

God gives us the gift of giving just like he gives us other gifts:

The Gift of the Ten Commandments

The Gift of Sex

The Gift of Family

The Gift of Freedom

The Gift of Grace

The Gift of Marriage

The Gift of Air

. . . and many others.

"Give and it will be given to you."

Interesting . . . If giving is a gift, why did Jesus have to *command* it? I mean, you don't have to be commanded to accept a gift, do you?

Answer: giving does not always come naturally to us and often must be pursued intentionally; therefore Jesus commands giving so we will practice it and enjoy its benefits.

The idea of "benefits" is more often associated with receiving than giving, but giving is associated with a whole array of positive results for the giver. Dr. Martin Seligman, a professor at the University of Pennsylvania, pioneered many of these findings in what he called "Lessons in Positive Psychology." Prior to this pioneering work and these "discoveries," Dr. Seligman said that psychology had largely dealt with negative issues of guilt, depression, anxiety, etc. Through controlled classroom studies, Dr. Seligman documented that (a) when students did good for others, it made them feel good, and (b) given this discovery of benevolence (students said), they would rather use their time and money to help others than play video games.

He wrote:

> *Enjoyment Versus Pleasure*
>
> In a similar vein, it is useful to distinguish positive experiences that are *pleasurable* from those that are enjoyable. Pleasure is the good feeling that comes from satisfying homeostatic needs such as hunger,

sex, and bodily comfort. Enjoyment, on the other hand, refers to the good feelings people experience when they break through the limits of homeostasis—when they do something that stretches them beyond what they were—in an athletic event, an artistic performance, a good deed, a stimulating conversation. Enjoyment, rather than pleasure, is what leads to personal growth and long-term happiness.

Like the fish who is unaware of the water in which it swims, people take for granted a certain amount of hope, love, enjoyment, and trust because these are the very conditions that allow them to go on living. These conditions are fundamental to existence, and if they are present, any number of obstacles can be faced with equanimity and even joy. [1]

What this tells us (and science proves) is that a lifestyle of giving is not only enjoyable but *life saving—for the giver!* When our minds and activities are wrapped around helping others, we are not self-absorbed (or depressed) with our own problems.

Dr. Seligman dramatized this truth by carrying out this classic experiment. Each student was told to perform a series of philanthropic activities, e.g., visiting shut-ins at a rest home, taking groceries to a homeless shelter, or volunteering as a reader at an inner-city school. They were also told to perform a series of "pleasurable" activities, e.g., going to a movie, surfing the Internet, or hanging out with friends.

"The results were dramatic," Dr. Seligman later reported. "The 'pleasurable' activity (hanging out with friends, going to a movie) paled in comparison to the effects of the kind action. When the philanthropic act was spontaneous and called upon skill, the rest of the day went better; whereas the pleasure of the pleasurable acts faded immediately. Positive Psychology taught me how I would like to live my life: put thought into every action, live purposefully and beautifully."

Great report, Dr. Seligman, and great inspiration. But it's not a "discovery." Jesus beat you by two thousand years when he said, "It is more blessed to give than to receive" (Acts 20:35). He knew that giving is far more than a nice gesture or a way to feel proud of oneself. Giving is intrinsically wrapped up in who we are, created in the image of God, the greatest Giver of all.

Giving Is the Cycle of Life Itself

Humans exhale CO_2, which plants inhale. Then, the plants give back, exhaling O_2, which humans inhale. Humans give back (again) by exhaling CO_2, which the plants inhale. And so the cycle continues. It's the cycle of nature, the cycle of giving, the cycle of life.

Giving/receiving, giving/receiving, giving/receiving.

Ponds, rivers, and oceans give their moisture to the sky to form clouds. The clouds give that moisture back to the earth in the form of rain and snow, which runs into those ponds, rivers, and oceans, which then give the moisture back to the clouds.

The cycle of water and rain and life continues.

Whether it is money, talent, time, energy, sweat, or affection, we give it, because *if we do not give,* we dry up and die. The gift of giving is commanded because the gift of giving *is* the gift of life.

Giving Snaps the Control Money Has Over Us

Giving snaps this fearful thought: *There won't be enough for me!*

When we see those dollar bills slip from our purse or pocket to be handed to another, hear the rip of the checkbook after writing a large and stunning check, or feel the slick plastic of the credit card as we hand it over to the treasurer of a charity, we enjoy a high. We experience hilarious joy and a feeling of freedom. Giving makes us feel free.

"Yes, there will be enough for me," we conclude as we give and give and give.

Giving Releases the Joy of Gratitude

The more we give, the more we are grateful for what we have. A geyser of gratitude erupts in us like Old Faithful. The attitude of gratitude drenches us with a sense of calm and peace. The attitude of gratitude is a gift that continues to come back *to us.*

As we saw in the last chapter, gratitude unlocks a whole host of benefits to nearly every aspect of a person's life: health, outlook, productivity, relationships, mind-set, and even lifespan.

Giving Takes Our Minds off Ourselves

Counselors tell us that the best way to take care of our problems is to help others with theirs.

Feeling lonely? Befriend a lonely person, and your loneliness will melt.

Feeling depressed? Lift up another, and your depression will fade.

Feeling scared? Encourage another, and you will soon find courage bubbling in your heart and mind.

Feeling broke? Give, give, give to others, and your fear of poverty will fade.

Giving Makes Us Feel Good

Clinical studies document that unconditional giving, i.e., *doing good without expectation of return*, delivers substantial benefits. Giving:

1. Releases positive chemical changes in the body.
2. Lowers blood pressure.
3. Calms the heart rate.
4. Delivers a healthy breathing pattern.
5. Rewards the giver with a sense of euphoria and heightened self-esteem.

Giving Is the Life of Christ

In northern England, there's a small village that still boasts a statue of Christ in the middle of the village. That statue and that town were bombed during World War II. When they rebuilt the town, they restored the statue of Christ and hoisted it in the middle of the square again. Instead of cementing the hands back on, the village leaders suggested leaving the hands off, with a plaque underneath: "Christ has no hands but ours."

Paul also described this opportunity and responsibility when he said, "It is no longer I who live, but Christ who lives through me."

Substantial, sacrificial, consistent giving helps others. This type of giving uniquely arises from following Jesus's examples and commands.

Let's imagine what Andy Angel might have said on the day Jesus ascended back to heaven. In wonder and astonishment, Andy stretches his wing out to nudge his buddy Alvin Angel.

"What's he doing back up here? We know he went down there to teach and to heal for three years and let those humans kill him, and he came back from the dead, and he taught them some more, and now he is back! But what is he doing up here? Why didn't he stay down there? After that resurrection, you know, he had a captive audience for the rest of his life, and for the whole earth. So why did he come back up here?"

Alvin explains: "He decided to leave the teaching of God's love to those humans. They would teach it, and live it, and show what the life of Christ was like."

Andy argues: "What? Those weak, fickle, scared, temperamental things down there called humans? *That's* the way the message of God's love to the human race and the entire earth is going to be given? That's how Jesus will deliver salvation, hope, money, goods, and services to that starving, desperate world?"

Alvin smiles and says: "There is no other way."

Right on: God's messages of hope and healing do not apply themselves. There is no other way.

Yes, God can heal the sick, feed the hungry, lift up the depressed, encourage the lonely, and rescue the lost directly if he chooses to do so. Instead, he chooses to recruit the sons of Adam and the daughters of Eve.

You and me.

We teach the love of Christ and apply his principles to human need.

Our world is packed with hospitals, schools, universities, shelters, and rescue missions with names like University of Notre Dame, Christ Chapel Food Bank, St. Louis University, Good Shepherd Rescue Mission, The Salvation Army, Chieng Mia Presbyterian Leprosy Hospital, Abilene Christian University, Deaconess Hospital, Methodist Health Systems, Lutheran Relief Missions, First Baptist Night Shelter, and thousands more. These shine the light of giving, of life and hope, in a dark world. As a prime example, here's the story of a normal Christian life, a life of giving with tears and laughter, the KLTY Chick-fil-A story:

Come to breakfast at a Chick-fil-A restaurant in the Dallas/Fort Worth area sometime between Thanksgiving and Christmas and you'll find KLTY (the nation's #1 Christian radio station) broadcasting live with its charitable champions Frank Reed, Bonnie Curry, Starlene Stringer, and others. They've got twenty thick, blue binders lined up around the restaurant, stuffed with hundreds of requests that, over the years, have attracted nearly a million dollars in gifts from KLTY listeners. Moms and dads, college students, engineers, physicians, programmers, CEOs, athletes . . . by the hundreds . . . grab a notebook and tear out a handful of requests, which they cheerfully fulfill.

One person helping another person. Unconditionally. The normal Christian life.

Requests sound like this:

> My dad lost his job three months ago. His company was bought out. He has looked every day—all day—for a job. Nothing. In the meantime, someone rear-ended him, and he's in pain all the time. He needs a good reliable car . . . the insurance won't nearly cover the cost of replacement, and our savings have run out. Is there someone out there who can provide a car? We also need about $2,000 to help pay the mortgage and keep food on the table for my brothers and sisters. There are four of us. My mother died several years ago. Thank you for understanding and thank you for any help you can provide.

And:

> We don't know where else to turn. Our church has helped as much as they can. Our grandmother— we call her Gram—had a stroke, and we brought her home to live with us. Our granddad—we call him Pappy—has been in the nursing home for

years with frontal brain dementia. Gram needs twenty-four-hour care, and for a lot of different reasons, she slips through the cracks of any government programs. Family and friends have filled in as much as we can, but we still need help. We live in Northwest Tarrant County, and we need about a dozen volunteers who will come and rotate at different times, just an hour or two at a time. We thank God in advance for you and for your help.

And they respond.

Hundreds of requests, hundreds of responses.

Bonnie Curry summarizes:

> Frank Reed was our trooper and got up every morning pretty sure that he'd be flying by the seat of his pants for those broadcasts. Well, our KLTY family came out in droves and "Christmas Wish" grew even more by allowing people to read the Wishes and grant them. Frank told me that a sweet lady came in one morning and quietly sat down with one of the books. She spent more than an hour reading through them. We found out later that she personally granted more than $12,000 worth of Wishes.
>
> Friends at Chick-fil-A became our permanent "Christmas Wish" home and we spent many a morning enjoying their delicious breakfasts and broadcasting live from all the corners of Dallas/Fort Worth. As usual, our KLTY family responded and more Wishes were granted and more clients came

on board to help us change lives. Today, we're still broadcasting from Chick-fil-A and thousands of people join us to grant Wishes . . . Every year, I sit down and read the Wishes that our interns have brought to our attention. And every year, my heart breaks just a little bit because the need is so great. Here's a little known fact: I'm famous for *not* crying. I hold it in as long as I can. My friend Frank Reed is such a tender-hearted person and the emotion and the tears you hear are very, very real. They come out spontaneously with Frank.

Last year, I visited the home of Carlissa to answer a Wish. She had cancer and when we met her, she seemed so fragile and weak. We recorded the wish the next day and were going to air it later that week, when a messenger walked into the studio when I was on the air. "Carlissa passed away last night." We decided to go ahead and air the Wish on KLTY to help provide for the many needs the family had. As I started working on the recording, my composure crumbled, and I cried on air. I listened to the sweet woman's voice, knowing she wasn't with us anymore, and I lost it. Tears rolled down my cheeks as I gave thanks to each and every person who had ever given to "Christmas Wish." In ten years, I've been privileged to see the very best in people because of Christian giving. I think I see the very best in people because of Christians being Christians and pouring out in unconditional giving.

Carlissa's son was blessed because of your generosity, KLTY family. His life was changed for the better because you gave.[2]

Christ, by his life and lips, and by his words and works, has inspired for centuries this type of sacrificial and substantial giving by Christians, both on a personal level and a public level.

The normal Christian life—a life of unconditional giving—was highlighted by Chick-fil-A founder S. Truett Cathy when he said, "Nearly every moment of every day, we have the opportunity to give something to someone else—our time, our love, our resources. I have always found more joy in giving when I did not expect anything in return."

Years ago, I was in the belly of the beast, earning my doctorate in the most liberal discipline, in the most liberal university. I heard the cynics: "You Christians give so you can earn your way to heaven. You Christians give to relieve guilt. You give for psychological egotism: to feel good about yourself."

Not so, my atheist friend. You do not understand grace. Christians are motivated by the grace of God. We gratefully accept his love and forgiveness, and therefore we are motivated to give love and forgiveness to others and to provide assistance wherever and whenever the need arises.

Warren Buffet spoke to the joy of giving and referenced the sacrificial habits of Christians—to give and give and give. Buffett's pledge puts in bold relief:

First, the joy of giving.

Second, the necessity of giving in order that the misery and suffering of others might be lifted.

We'll look at Buffett's charitable pledge in its entirety and then examine the dynamics of his pledge and how his statements apply to the divine gift called *giving*.

$\bowtie$

My Philanthropic Pledge
By Warren Buffett

In 2006, I made a commitment to gradually give all of my Berkshire Hathaway stock to philanthropic foundations. I couldn't be happier with that decision.

Now Bill and Melinda Gates and I are asking hundreds of rich Americans to pledge at least 50 percent of their wealth to charity. So I think it is fitting that I reiterate my intentions and explain the thinking that lies behind them.

First, my pledge: More than 99 percent of my wealth will go to philanthropy during my lifetime or at death. Measured by dollars, this commitment is large. In a comparative sense, however, many individuals give more to others every day.

Millions of people who regularly contribute to churches, schools, and other organizations thereby relinquish the use of funds that would otherwise benefit their own families. The dollars these people drop into a collection plate or give to United Way mean forgone movies, dinners out, or other personal pleasures. In contrast, my family and I will give up nothing we need or want by fulfilling this 99 percent pledge.

Moreover, my pledge does not leave me contributing the most precious asset, which is *time*. Many people, including—I'm proud to say—my three children, give extensively of their own time and talents to help others. Gifts of this kind often prove far more valuable than money. A struggling child, befriended and nurtured by a caring mentor, receives a gift whose value far exceeds what can be bestowed by a check. My sister, Doris, extends significant person-to-person help daily. I've done little of this.

What I can do, however, is to take a pile of Berkshire Hathaway stock certificates—"claim checks" that when converted to cash can command far-ranging resources—and commit them to benefit others . . . To date about 20 percent of my shares have been distributed (including shares given by my late wife, Susan Buffett). I will continue to annually distribute about 4 percent of the shares I retain. At the latest, the proceeds from all of my Berkshire shares will be expended for philanthropic purposes by ten years after my estate is settled. Nothing will go to endowments; I want the money spent on current needs.

This pledge will leave my lifestyle untouched and that of my children as well. They have already received significant sums for their personal use and will receive more in the future. They live comfortable and productive lives. I will continue to live in a manner that gives me everything that I could possibly want in life.

Some material things make my life more enjoyable; many, however, would not. I like having an expensive private plane, but owning a half-dozen homes would be a burden. Too often, a vast collection of possessions ends up possessing its owner. The asset I most value, aside from health, is interesting, diverse, and long-standing friends.

My wealth has come from a combination of living in America, some lucky genes, and compound interest. Both my children and I won what I call the ovarian lottery. (For starters, the odds against my birth taking place in the United States were at least 30 to 1. . . .)

The reaction of my family and me to our extraordinary good fortune is not guilt, but rather gratitude. Were we to use more than 1 percent of my claim checks on ourselves, neither our happiness nor our well-being would be enhanced. In contrast, that remaining 99 percent can have a huge effect on the health and welfare of others. That reality sets an obvious course for me and my family: Keep all we can conceivably need and distribute the rest to society, for its needs. My pledge starts us down that course.

Buffett's Pledge magnifies the teachings of Jesus in many ways:

1. "I made a commitment to gradually give all of my Berkshire Hathaway stock to philanthropic foundations. I couldn't be *happier* with that decision."

Like Rex Harrison said to Audrey Hepburn in *My Fair Lady*: "By Jove, she's got it. I believe she's got it!"
Warren Buffett has got it.
Giving makes people feel happy. This is the truth of Acts 20:35: "It is more blessed to give than to receive."

Giving without ulterior motives makes one ecstatic. Now that's *not* the reason we give. But it is a welcome serendipity.

2. Buffett also said, "Measured by dollars, this commitment is large. In a comparative sense, however, many individuals give more to others every day."

Right on, Warren.

Jesus spoke of this when he talked about one's attitude and one's circumstances in regard to giving. He praised the widow with the two coins: "But a poor widow came and put in two very small copper coins, worth only a few cents. He called his disciples to him and said, 'That poor widow has given more than all those rich men put together, for they gave a little of their extra fat where she gave up her last penny'" (Mark 12:42–44).

In a comparative sense, she gave more than others.

3. Buffett praises and acknowledges the dynamics of sacrificial giving:

> "Millions of people who regularly contribute to churches, schools, and other organizations thereby relinquish the use of funds that would otherwise benefit their own families. The dollars these people drop into a collection plate or give to United Way mean forgone movies, dinners out, or other personal pleasures."

This truth is dramatized many places in the New Testament, including the teachings of Paul, where he said: "In the midst of a very severe trial, their overflowing joy and their extreme poverty welled up in rich generosity" (2 Cor. 8:2).

4. Buffett's wealth is not going to casinos, to cruise ships, to enrich a zillion-dollar trust for his kids, or to build bigger and bigger businesses. This statement is reflective of what Jesus said in Luke 12:16–21:

> And he told them this parable:
>
> The ground of a certain rich man yielded an abundant harvest. He thought to himself, "What shall I do? I have no place to store my crops."
>
> Then he said, "This is what I'll do. I will tear down my barns and build bigger ones, and there I will store my surplus grain. And I'll say to myself, 'You have plenty of grain laid up for many years. Take life easy; eat, drink, and be merry.'"
>
> But God said to him, "You fool! This very night your life will be demanded from you. Then who will get what you have prepared for yourself?"
>
> This is how it will be with whoever stores up things for themselves but is not rich toward God." (Luke 12:16–21)

5. Finally, Warren praises those who give their time:

> "My pledge does not leave me contributing the most precious asset, which is *time*. Many people, including—I'm proud to say—my three children, give extensively of their own time and talents to help others. Gifts of this kind often prove far more valuable than money. A struggling child, befriended

and nurtured by a caring mentor, receives a gift whose value far exceeds what can be bestowed by a check."

With regards to earning money, time is like the manna that God rained on the Israelites during their wandering. He told them to eat it up every day because the next day it would not be good. They could not store it for tomorrow.

There are numerous ways to give of yourself—money, time, energy, love, friendship, prayer, and many more—and just as many benefits that you will enjoy in the process. Each morning, the sun rises and gives us another twenty-four hours to make a difference in someone else's life and to reap the rewards in our own.

How can you give of yourself today?

Notes

1. Martin E. P. Seligman, "Positive Psychology: An Introduction," *American Psychologist* 55.1 (January 2000): 5–14.
2. From "10 Year Anniversary Christmas Wish" by Bonnie Curry, December 2012.

2

Jesus on Money

2a. Don't Love It

2b. Do Give It

Part One: The Gift of Giving

Part Two: Are You a Flint, Sponge, or Honeycomb?

2c. How to Earn It

Part One: Employee

Part Two: Self-Employed

Part Three: Business Leader: The Boss

2d. How to Make It Grow: Power, Profit, Peace of Mind, and Putting People First

Part One: Jesus on Growing Money

Part Two: Jesus's Talent Parable

Part Three: Jesus's Tower Parable

Part Four: The Tower Parable and the Power of Critical Reasoning

Part Five: Jesus's Mustard Seed Parable: Let My Money Grow

Part Six: Jesus on Taxes

Do Give It

Are You a Flint,
Sponge, or Honeycomb?

When many people hear the word "tithe," which means giving at least one-tenth of one's income back to God, they think of an outdated religious practice with no real application to modern-day life. Or perhaps they think uncomfortably of churches passing the collection plate. Some may automatically think, *Isn't that an Old Testament rule we don't have to follow anymore now that we're covered by grace?* The truth is that tithing is an incredible financial opportunity and a blessing to the giver.

In fact, the benefits of tithing were put to the test in modern times in two famous stories reported in *Time* magazine on July 26, 1943 and July 30, 1945. The first one was entitled "Parable Proved" and the second was titled "Dynamic Kernels."

The short version is this:

Perry Hayden, a Quaker, was a miller who lived in Tecumseh, Michigan. One Sunday, he heard two sermons that grabbed his attention. The sermons were based upon two Bible verses. The first was Malachi 3:10: "'Bring the whole tithe into the storehouse, that there may be food in my house. Test me in this,' says the LORD Almighty, 'and see if I will not throw open the floodgates of heaven and pour out so much blessing that there will not be room enough to store it.'" The second was John 12:24: "'Very truly I tell you, unless a kernel of wheat falls to the ground and dies, it remains only a single seed. But if it dies, it produces many seeds.'"

Hayden decided to test God's wisdom and see for himself if these two teachings worked, so he launched an experiment. The first thing he did was to sow a field for six years and let it rest the seventh year, based upon another scripture that he took seriously: "For six years sow your fields, and for six years prune your vineyards and gather their crops. But in the seventh year the land is to have a year of Sabbath rest, a Sabbath to the LORD. Do not sow your fields or prune your vineyards" (Lev. 25:3–4).

Results:

Year one: September 26, 1940. He planted 360 kernels into a four-foot-by-eight-foot plot of land. He announced to all present that he would be tithing 10 percent of the crop when he harvested the following year and they would replant the remaining kernels.

Year two: Summer of 1941. The *first harvest* yielded fifty cubic inches of wheat. Hayden tithed 10 percent to his local church and planted the remaining forty-five cubic inches in September 1941.

Year three: Summer of 1942. The *second harvest* exploded, yielding seventy *pounds* of wheat. This yield was fifty-five-fold. He tithed 10 percent, for the third year in a row, and planted sixty-three pounds of seed on land now provided by Henry Ford.

Year four: Summer of 1943. The *third harvest* exploded even more, yielding sixteen *bushels* of wheat. This time, Henry Ford attended the harvest and brought machinery of his own to help with the harvesting. Mr. Ford graciously agreed to provide additional land for the growing experiment, which would require fourteen acres to plant the seed for next year's crop. Again, 10 percent of the harvest was tithed, and the remaining seed was planted.

Year five: Summer of 1944. The *fourth harvest* yielded 380 bushels of wheat. By now the seed being planted had been given the name Dynamic Kernels by the media. Again, 10 percent was tithed, and this time it took 230 acres of Ford's land to plant the crop.

Year six: Summer of 1945. The *fifth harvest* yielded 5,555 bushels of wheat. The value of this fifth crop was set at market price, which was $1.55 per bushel, making the total market value $8,610.25. A total of $861.03 went to Mr. Hayden's local church as his tithe, and they, in turn, donated it to their local hospital. This was to be the sixth year of planting for the remaining five thousand bushels of wheat. The harvest had been so expansive that the wheat had to be sold to twenty-seven farmers in order for the wheat to be planted. They represented thirty religious faiths, and the planting required 2,666 acres of land. All of the farmers agreed to tithe 10 percent to their own churches.

Year seven: The *sixth harvest* yielded 72,150 bushels of wheat worth approximately $150,000, and a large portion of this tithe was sent to Europe for famine relief. The governor at that time proclaimed August 1, 1946, to be "Biblical Wheat Day."

Hayden concluded the experiment by announcing to all what Henry Ford had said at the end of their experiment: "I believe the lesson we taught on tithing at Tecumseh, Michigan, will eclipse any of my other accomplishments."

Ford was right. Many lessons erupt from the practice of tithing:

1. Tithing motivates greater faithfulness for oneself and others.
2. Tithing releases God's financial blessings.
3. Tithing expands God's work.
4. Tithes and offerings are part of the New Testament challenge, as well as the Old Testament commandments.
5. Tithing changes spending habits.
6. Tithing brings people closer because they have a common purpose.

Eventually, the person who tithes will realize the promises of Proverbs 11:23–25: "One person gives freely, yet gains even more; another withholds unduly, but comes to poverty. A generous person will prosper; whoever refreshes others will be refreshed."

The principle and power of tithing is still with us. When people tithe today, they give at least 10 percent, empowering them with the joys of tithing described above. As we examine tithing, we might helpfully consider three types of givers: the Flint, the Sponge, and the Honeycomb.

The Flint: You strike real hard to get this person to let off any spark of giving.

The Sponge: You have to squeeze real hard to get this person to release any time or money.

The Honeycomb: Ah, the honeycomb. It gives sweetness to all who encounter it, as if that is all it was made to do. The honeycomb is a picture of hilarious giving, which Jesus applauds and which was originally dramatized in the practice of tithing. Tithing is commanded in the Old Testament: give the best of what you've got, meaning the first fruits, the cream of the crop, the first 10 percent or better. God commanded tithing because he knew there would be flints and sponges. He knew that some people would never experience the joy of sacrificial giving *unless* he commanded its practice.

> Speak to the Levites and say to them: "When you receive from the Israelites the tithe I give you as your inheritance, you must present a tenth of that tithe as the LORD's offering." (Num. 18:26)

> As soon as the order went out, the Israelites generously gave the first fruits of their grain, new wine, olive oil and honey and all that the fields produced. They brought a great amount, a tithe of everything. (2 Chron. 31:5)

> "Concerning tithes and offerings, you are under a curse—your whole nation—because you are robbing me. Bring the whole tithe into the storehouse, that there may be food in my house. Test me in this,"

says the Lord Almighty, "and see if I will not throw open the floodgates of heaven and pour out so much blessing that there will not be room enough to store it." (Mal. 3:8–10)

"At the end of every three years, bring all the tithes of that year's produce and store it in your towns . . ." (Deut. 14:28)

Jesus and Tithing

Although Jesus did not command tithing, he definitely encouraged its practice:

> Woe to you, teachers of the law and Pharisees, you hypocrites! You give a tenth of your spices—mint, dill, and cumin. But you have neglected the more important matters of the law—justice, mercy, and faithfulness. You should have practiced the latter, without neglecting the former. (Matt. 23:23)

> Woe to you Pharisees, because you give God a tenth of your mint, rue, and all other kinds of garden herbs, but you neglect justice and the love of God. You should have practiced the latter without leaving the former undone. (Luke 11:42)

Jesus never commanded his followers to enjoy the practice of fasting, either. He acknowledged its presence and assumed that his followers would embrace it: "When you fast, do not look somber as the hypocrites do, for they disfigure their faces to show others they are fasting.

Truly I tell you, they have received their reward in full" (Matt. 6:16).

Jesus also wanted (and wants) his followers to enjoy life *to the full*: "The thief comes only to steal and kill and destroy; I have come that they may have life, and have it to the full" (John 10:10).

Jesus assumed that in response to our grateful embrace of the abundant life, we would gladly give 10 percent and a whole lot more. It is indicative of Jesus's teachings: "Do not think that I have come to abolish the Law or the Prophets; I have not come to abolish them but to fulfill them" (Matt. 5:17). Fulfilling them means people respond to God's grace not with reluctant and resentful obedience but with outrageous joy and visible gratitude.

It is the difference between law and grace.

In the pioneer days of the Old West, a pitiful woman was married to a cruel and brutal rancher. He demanded she rise at 4:00 a.m. to milk the cows, feed the chickens, help round up the strays, and a variety of other back-breaking chores before she returned to the house at 6:00 a.m. to fix him a massive breakfast. Then each day, he had a variety of other chores for her to do before he returned, demanding a massive lunch. The afternoon was the same—more sweat-busting work before she prepared a massive supper. While doing all this, she was to keep their house immaculate, which was very difficult in their windswept, dusty cabin. She hated her job and her life. But it was his *law*. It was painful to drag her tired body out of bed each morning, and painful to perform the slavish tasks of farming, ranching, cooking, cleaning, hauling water, etc.

Brute husband died, and she married a man who was kind, gentle, supportive, and appreciative. She found herself again rising at 4:00 a.m., going with him for the milking, feeding, hauling water—and she loved it. She found herself doing it automatically and cheerfully.

The difference this time was that she was doing it out of gratitude and grace. She enjoyed the morning and afternoon chores. She enjoyed fixing the meals . . . for the man she loved.

Here is the contrast Jesus taught and dramatized in his life:

Law (Old Testament)	Grace (New Testament)
• Obey the law, every word. Obey the letter of the law, not the spirit of the law. • Fear is the motivator. • Rules are primary.	• Fulfill the Law, Expand it, Enrich it, Dramatize it . . . With love and service. • Love is the motivator. • A relationship with God is primary.

Jesus came:

1. To show us that the Ten Commandments were gifts from God, i.e., rules to protect us from destroying ourselves and others.

   and

2. To show us that it was the spirit behind the Ten Commandments that was primary, enriching, and liberating.

The legendary R. J. LeTourneau dramatized the honey-comb principle.

LeTourneau built his empire of earthmoving equipment into abundant wealth. It is he for whom LeTourneau University is named. He gave away 90 percent of his money, and his giving continues to bless people today. Most of us will probably not be in a position to give away 90 percent of our income, but we can take a serious look at the principle of tithing and the many blessings that result from faithful giving.

In *Mover of Man and Mountains*, LeTourneau wrote:

> To what foolish lengths man will let his pride drive him. God does not do business that way. He keeps his promises. When you ask his help, he doesn't answer that he has a lot of pressing things to attend to, so come back next year. His time is *now*. In the early days, the true Christians gave God his share from the *first fruits* of their crops. They had faith. They didn't wait around to see if the crops were to be destroyed by locusts or drought. *Let God's will be done and the rewards will be so great that there won't be room to store them.* But start to hedge, and wait to see how the whole crop turns out before giving God his share, and he knows you as a man of little faith . . .[1]

I'd like to share with you one more example of the honeycomb principle in action, one that illustrates the hilarious joy of giving. Each year about Christmas time, this story circulates on the Internet.[2]

Too bad.

Too bad it's only at Christmas time that it is passed around.

Are you ready?

Grab a Kleenex. No, a bath towel . . . you'll need it for the tears of triumph and joy.

It was Christmas Eve 1881. I was fifteen years old and feeling like the world had caved in on me because there just hadn't been enough money to buy me the rifle that I'd wanted for Christmas.

We did the chores early that night for some reason. I just figured Pa wanted a little extra time so we could read in the Bible. After supper was over I took my boots off and stretched out in front of the fireplace. I was still feeling sorry for myself and, to be honest, I wasn't in much of a mood to read scriptures. But Pa didn't get the Bible, instead he bundled up again and went outside. I couldn't figure it out because we had already done all the chores. I didn't worry about it long, though; I was too busy wallowing in self-pity.

Soon Pa came back in. It was a cold, clear night out, and there was ice in his beard. "Come on, Matt," he said. "Bundle up good, it's cold out tonight."

I was really upset then. Not only wasn't I getting the rifle for Christmas, now Pa was dragging me out in the cold, and for no earthly reason that I could see. But I knew Pa was not very patient at one dragging one's feet when he'd told them to do something, so I got up and put my boots back on and got my cap, coat, and mittens. Ma gave me a mysterious smile as I opened the door to leave the house. Something was up, but I didn't know what.

Outside, I became even more dismayed. There in front of the house was the work team, already hitched to the big sled. Whatever it was we were going to do wasn't going to be a quick job. We never hitched up this sled unless we were going to haul a big load. Pa was already up on the seat, reins in hand. I reluctantly climbed up beside him.

The cold was already biting at me. I wasn't happy. When I was on, Pa pulled the sled around the house and stopped in front of the woodshed. He got off and I followed.

"I think we'll put on the high sideboards," he said. "Here, help me."

The high sideboards! It had been a bigger job than I wanted to do with just the low sideboards on. After we had exchanged the sideboards, Pa went into the woodshed and came out with an armload of wood—the wood I'd spent all summer hauling down from the mountain, and then all fall sawing into blocks and splitting.

Finally I said something. "Pa, what are you doing?"

"You been by the Widow Jensen's lately?" he asked. The Widow Jensen lived about two miles down the road. Her husband had died a year or so before and left her with three children, the oldest being eight. Sure, I'd been by, but so what?

"Yeah," I said, "Why?"

"I rode by just today. Little Jakey was out digging around in the woodpile trying to find a few chips. They're out of wood, Matt." That was all he said, and then he turned and went back into the woodshed for another armload of wood. I followed him. We loaded the sled so high that I began to wonder if the horses would be able to pull it.

Finally, Pa called a halt to our loading, then we went to the smoke house and Pa took down a big ham and a side of bacon. He handed them to me and told me to put them in the sled and wait. When he returned he was carrying a sack of flour over his right shoulder and a smaller sack of something in his left hand.

"What's in the little sack?"

"Shoes. Little Jakey just had gunny sacks wrapped around his feet when he was out in the woodpile this morning. I got the children a little candy, too. It just wouldn't be Christmas without a little candy."

We rode the two miles to Widow Jensen's pretty much in silence. I tried to think through what Pa was doing. We didn't have much by worldly standards. Of course, we did have a big woodpile, though most of what was left now was still in the form of logs that I would have to saw into blocks and split before we could use it. We also had meat and flour, so we could spare that, but I knew we didn't have any money, so why was Pa buying them shoes and candy? Really, why was he doing any of this? Widow Jensen had closer neighbors than us; it shouldn't have been our concern.

We came in from the blind side of the Jensen house and unloaded the wood as quietly as possible, then we took the meat and flour and shoes to the door. We knocked. The door opened a crack and a timid voice said, "Who is it?"

"Lucas Miles, Ma'am, and my son, Matt. Could we come in for a bit?"

Widow Jensen opened the door and let us in. She had a blanket wrapped around her shoulders. The children were wrapped in another and were sitting in front of the fireplace by a very small fire that hardly gave off any heat at all. Widow Jensen fumbled with a match and finally lit the lamp.

"We brought you a few things, Ma'am," Pa said and set down the sack of flour. I put the meat on the table. Then Pa handed her the sack that had the shoes in it. She opened it hesitantly and took the shoes out one pair at a time. There was a pair for her and one for each of the children—sturdy shoes, the best, shoes that would last. I watched her carefully. She bit her lower lip to keep it from trembling and then tears filled her eyes and started running down her cheeks. She looked up at Pa like she wanted to say something, but it wouldn't come out.

"We brought a load of wood, too, Ma'am," Pa said. He turned to me and said, "Matt, go bring in enough to last awhile. Let's get that fire up to size and heat this place up."

I wasn't the same person when I went back out to bring in the wood. I had a big lump in my throat, and as much as I hate to admit it, there were tears in my eyes, too. In my mind I kept seeing those three kids huddled around the fireplace and their mother standing there with so much gratitude in her heart that she couldn't speak.

My heart swelled within me and a joy that I'd never known before filled my soul. I had given at Christmas many times before, but never when it had made so much difference. I could see we were literally saving the lives of these people.

I soon had the fire blazing and everyone's spirits soared. The kids started giggling when Pa handed them each a piece of candy and Widow Jensen looked on with a smile that probably hadn't crossed her face for a long time. She finally turned to us. "God bless you," she said. "I know the Lord has sent you. The children and I have been praying that he would send one of his angels to spare us."

In spite of myself, the lump returned to my throat. I'd never thought of Pa in those exact terms before, but after Widow Jensen mentioned it I could see that it was probably true. I was sure that a better man than Pa had never walked the earth. I started remembering all the times he had gone out of his way for Ma and me, and many others. The list seemed endless as I thought on it.

Pa insisted that everyone try on the shoes before we left. I was amazed when they all fit and I wondered how he had known what sizes to get. Then I guessed that if he was on an errand for the Lord that the Lord would make sure he got the right sizes.

Tears were running down Widow Jensen's face again when we stood up to leave. Pa took each of the kids in his big arms and gave them a hug. They clung to him and didn't want us to go. I could see that they missed their Pa and I was glad that I still had mine.

At the door, Pa turned to Widow Jensen and said, "The Mrs. wanted me to invite you and the children over for Christmas dinner tomorrow. The turkey will be more than the three of us can eat, and a man can get cantankerous if he has to eat turkey for too many meals. We'll be by to get you about eleven. It'll be nice to have some little ones around again. Matt, here, hasn't been little for quite a spell." I was the youngest. My two brothers and two sisters had all married and moved away.

Widow Jensen nodded. "Thank you, Brother Miles. I don't have to say, 'May the Lord bless you,' I know for certain that he will."

Out on the sled I felt a warmth that came from deep within and I didn't even notice the cold. When we had gone a ways, Pa turned to me. "Matt, I want you to know something. Your ma and me have been tucking a little money away here and there all year so we could buy that rifle for you, but we didn't have quite enough. Then yesterday a man who owed me a little money from years back came by to make things square. Your ma and me were real excited, thinking that now we could get you that rifle, and I started into town this morning to do just that, but on the way I saw little Jakey out scratching in the woodpile with his feet wrapped in those gunny sacks and I knew what I had to do. Son, I spent the money for shoes and a little candy for those children. I hope you understand."

I understood very well, and my eyes became wet with tears again. Now the rifle seemed very low on my list of priorities. Pa had given me a lot more. He had given me the look on Widow Jensen's face and the radiant smiles of her three children. For the rest of my life, whenever I saw any of the Jensens, or split a block of wood, I remembered, and remembering brought back that same joy I felt riding home beside Pa that night. Pa had given me much more than a rifle that night, he had given me the best Christmas of my life.

All the joys of giving taught by Jesus are here:

1. Giving is often inconvenient, even painful at the moment. "I was too busy wallowing in self-pity." "The cold was already biting at me. I wasn't happy."
2. Giving fills a need. "I could see we were literally saving the lives of these people. I soon had the fire in place and everyone's spirits soared."
3. Giving makes us feel good. "Pa had given me much more than a rifle, he had given me the best Christmas of my life."
4. The blessings of giving go on and on and on. "Pa had given me the look on Widow Jensen's face and the radiant smiles of her three children. For the rest of my life . . . I remembered . . . that same joy I felt riding home beside Pa that night."

Giving is pure joy.

Thank you, God, for the gift of giving, and thank you, Jesus, for dramatizing it by your lips and life and giving us the opportunity to demonstrate it, also.

Notes

1. R.G. LeTourneau, *Mover of Men and Mountains* (Chicago: Moody Press, 1972), 173.
2. Author unknown, condensed here.

Jesus on Money

How to Earn It

Introduction: Work and Money

The worker deserves his wages.

—1 Timothy 5:18

In contemporary American culture, two views of work dominate popular perception:

1. Work is a necessary evil.
2. Work defines who I am.

These views, which are dark and depressing, stand in sharp contrast to the view of work that God desires us to have.

Trapped by the attitude that "work is a necessary evil," a person grumbles: "Got to show up. Thirty more years. Hate the job. Hate the commute. Hate the boss. Hate the customers. Hate co-workers. Hate to suck up and show up every day."

So, with the acid of anger spraying in her stomach and daggers of pain stabbing her neck and shoulders, she stumbles to work, hanging on with "just thirty years to go."

"Just twenty-five."
"Just eighteen."
"Just nine."
Etc.

The daily mantra: "If I can just make it to retirement . . . then I will be happy."

This is not an attitude of work that embraces and enjoys the teachings of Jesus Christ.

No joy, zest, pride, or gratitude.

I know there's a need for retirement planning. I am a financial counselor and retirement planner.

But I also know the words "retire" or "retirement" do not appear in the Bible.

Surprised?

God expects us—check that—*allows* us to be creative and productive *all our lives.*

I tell clients, "Let's use the word *recycle* rather than retire. I'll help you recycle into a new and challenging set of opportunities. Let's use your pension, IRA rollover, and social security as your base of financial support and find something that is fulfilling . . . whether you get paid or not."

We were made to work, grow, and create. All our lives.

No doubt you heard about that study where experimenters enlisted volunteers to test a human's response to total relaxation, absent of any resistance. Experimenters put the subjects in a pool of water at 98.6 degrees Fahrenheit. Perfect body temp. They plugged their ears and snapped floaters on their chests, arms, and ankles. They blindfolded them and attached oxygen masks, allowing them to lie face down in a bed of warm water. Subjects had no sense of sensation other than the automatic intake of oxygen.

Experimenters smashed the project within minutes. With no stimulation or sensation, subjects were going crazy.

Conclusion: The human mind and body need challenge and resistance, the kind we get with WORK.

One poster says, "SHIPS ARE SAFE IN THE HARBOR, BUT THAT'S NOT WHAT SHIPS ARE MADE FOR."

Workers (like you and me) like the dream of retirement, but that is not what we were made for. With new challenges, people discover the senior years—the so-called "retirement years"—are not only golden years but are also go-go years, opening up new avenues for work and service.

The other extreme is "Work defines who I am." With this attitude,

- The greater my income.
- The richer my portfolio.
- The fatter my wallet.
- The bigger my collection of cars, jewelry, and homes.
- The thicker my résumé of awards, degrees, and positive press.
- The "better" person I am.

This is the attitude of the rich man in Luke 18:18–23:

A certain ruler asked him, "Good teacher, what must I do to inherit eternal life?"

"Why do you call me good?" Jesus answered. "No one is good—except God alone. You know the commandments: 'You shall not commit adultery, you shall not murder, you shall not steal, you shall not give false testimony, honor your father and mother.'"

"All these I have kept since I was a boy," he said.

When Jesus heard this, he said to him, "You still lack one thing. Sell everything you have and give to the poor, and you will have treasure in heaven. Then come, follow me."

When he heard this, he became very sad, because he was very wealthy.

From the rich man's point of view, when his money was taken away, his life was taken away.

By contrast, the healthy and biblical approach to work is "If money were no object, what kind of work would I do for the rest of my life?"

And do it!

"That's unrealistic, Dr. Gallagher."

Maybe it is right now, but write a plan to embrace that passion. Invest your energies in something you know is worthwhile and personally fulfilling. Invest your life into a task or a project that will inspire others to gasp, "I didn't know you could do that!"

"The Worker Is Worthy of His Hire"

The lips and life of Jesus blast an urgent message to an American culture of apathy and mediocrity characterized by "Do as little as you can, for as short a time as you can, and get paid as much as you can." The mantra of millions.

Sad:

Sad for the worker,

Sad for his family,

Sad for his company,

Sad for the country.

Two-thirds of Jesus's parables talk about earning money through diligent work.

Go to work.

Jesus worked.

A carpenter in his time, he was, in fact, a craftsman:

> Who, after all, can imagine Jesus turning out shoddy work? The Biblical term for *carpenter* suggests a craftsman. In the earlier days, and still today in many places, in small towns like Nazareth, there were village craftsmen, handymen who could repair a gate, build useful cabinets, or make a set of table and chairs. That is the kind of work Jesus did. The drawers of the cabinets ran smoothly, the yokes were well balanced, the boxes were square, and the toys were sturdy and safe.[1]

Mel Gibson, in *The Passion of the Christ*, stretched our imaginations by showing teen Jesus helping dad Joseph in his craft as a carpenter building (what we call today) a bar stool, i.e., a raised chair with solid legs and arms.

But it does not take imagination to read Jesus's words and feel Jesus's attitudes about work and earning money:

- In his parables, Jesus praised diligent, loyal, and grateful workers.
- He scolded the lazy and envious workers.
- Jesus described himself as a workman who was sent to take care of the vineyard.
- Jesus accomplished the *works* of his Father. (John 4:34, 5:17, 5:36, 10:32–37, 14:10–13, 17:4)

And he chose leaders familiar with work. When choosing a leader and worker, Jesus did not look at a person's ability or inability. He looked at their *availability* to lead and their *attitude* toward work.

When Jesus chose a worker named Peter, he found in him:

- Available hands and a hard body, sculpted from decades of hard work as a sun-baked fisherman.
- An attitude of heart and mind that was eager to say, "Lord, to whom shall we go? You have the words of eternal life." (John 6:68)

And, after a brief, tragic, and remorseful defection, Peter (like Rocky in the ring) roared back to attack Christ's crucifiers:

> This man was handed over to you by God's deliberate plan and foreknowledge; and you, with the help

of wicked men, put him to death by nailing him to the cross. (Acts 2:23)

Therefore let all Israel be assured of this: God has made this Jesus, whom you crucified, both Lord and Messiah. (Acts 2:36)

Later, this same leader said, "We must obey God rather than human beings!" (Acts 5:29). Peter's training as a tough worker and loyal follower of Christ erupted into his fearless and passionate proclamation of the gospel.

Then there was Paul, the worker missionary. Paul built tents. Paul walked the globe preaching. Paul was a leader with an intense goal, strong physique, and an iron character of endurance forged by . . . work. Paul is the one who said:

But by the grace of God I am what I am, and his grace to me was not without effect. No, I worked harder than all of them—yet not I, but the grace of God that was with me. (1 Cor. 15:10)

Whatever you do, work at it with all your heart, as working for the Lord, not for human masters . . . (Col. 3:23)

For even when we were with you, we gave you this rule: 'The one who is unwilling to work shall not eat." (2 Thess. 3:10)

. . . and to make it your ambition to lead a quiet life: You should mind your own business and work with your hands, just as we told you . . . (1 Thess. 4:11)

The Lord found in Paul, like Peter, an *availability* to lead and a positive *attitude* toward work. We are all like Paul and Peter in that we all have skills and talents, and it's a compliment to us that God calls us to stretch those skills and talents when we display our own healthy availability and attitude.

Prior to demonstrating the dignity of work through the life and lips of Jesus and his followers, God blessed the beauty and dignity of work with Old Testament dignitaries. God even told Adam and Eve to work. He told them to take care of the garden. This was *before* they sinned and *before* the fall.

Therefore, it is *not* true that work is a curse and a burden to mankind as a result of the fall. Genesis 2:5 shows that God planned work from the very beginning as part of his creative process.

Work is a gift.

God lavished the gift of work upon Adam and Eve because of its many benefits, which I summarize here as the six big C's:

- Community
- Commitment
- Courage
- Compassion
- Creativity
- Contribution

Unless you're living on an island like the legendary Robinson Crusoe, work is done in the context of *community*. To be meaningful or productive, work requires *commitment*. Whether working for yourself or someone else, it also requires *courage* to believe that what you are doing will be appreciated and rewarded. Work involves *compassion*—the end result of any product or service is people, and compassion is one of the forces that drives you. Work involves *creativity*, the opportunity to bring something into the world that did not exist before. Finally, work involves *contribution*. In survey after survey, when employees were given ten criteria of what they want most in their workplace—salary, benefits, vacation, etc.—overwhelmingly, the number one preference, beyond even salary and benefits, was freedom on the job to use their talents. Closely aligned with that was a sense of significance, that what they were doing was useful.

You can take the attitude "You take this job and shove it," or you can take the attitude "I'll take this job and love it." What makes the discipline of work unique to the Christian is that there's a tension in the Christian's sense of service. There's a passion for profit and a passion for progress, but these are balanced with a passion for people. People are more important than profits, and relationships are more important than revenue.

Where there is no God, all things are possible. Many writers have said this, and it certainly applies in the workplace. Where there is no God, then profit is the singular and all-consuming drive. The Christian has to maintain a balance and pursue profit for the purpose of helping people. This is the invisible hand of compassion in capitalism.

The Christian worker, recognizing the gift of work, takes the attitude described by Louis L'Amour in his *Riding for the Brand*. When you're riding for the brand, you give your trail boss and the ranch owner all you have. You don't, on the side, work for another outfit. You're riding for the brand. What that means for the Christian worker is that you begin every day praying, "Lord, help me to anticipate other people's needs—other people in the office, the customers' needs, the suppliers' needs—everyone is important, everyone. The janitor, the mailman, the FedEx delivery person, the president of the company, as well as the fifty other people who work in cubicles. Everyone is important." The Christian worker prays every day to anticipate other people's needs and meet those needs throughout the day.

At one of the nation's major nursing schools, the final exam includes a surprise question. After asking questions about molecular structure, clinical trials, and a variety of issues important to nursing, the final question is *What is the name of the lady who comes in at night to clean the sink and empty the wastebaskets?* A lot of students think it's a joke, but it's not. What the examiner is concerned with, and what the nursing student needs to find out, is that every person is important. Every person has a name, a history, needs, hopes, a need for recognition, and so on.

The attitude of the Christian is this: when you do what you love, people will love what you do. They will flock to your company and to your product. People can feel that you have a passion for excellence and for service.

Regard your work with the attitude that even if you were not getting paid, you would still be doing this job, and if you don't feel that enthusiastic about it, then you better get yourself to a place where you are! Make yourself see over and over again the benefits of what you're providing, and if there's someplace else that you'll feel more fulfilled, there's nothing wrong with looking for that while you're doing your best at the job that you're in.

If you're in a supervisor position in the workforce, you understand the truth that Einstein stated: "Imagination is more important than knowledge." People want to be able to use their imaginations to improve their product or service and to improve themselves in the workplace. Give them that freedom; give them that encouragement.

In order to maintain the balance between profit, progress, and putting people first, the Christian prays at the beginning of every working day, "God, make my life a miracle of your service today. Honor me by sending me impossible tasks, so that when I complete those tasks You will get the credit and the glory." Sometimes, that means just waiting, waiting while you're improving your skills or your opportunity. John Milton wrote,

> God doth not need
> Either man's work or his own gifts: who best
> Bear his mild yoke, they serve him best. His state
> Is kingly; thousands at his bidding speed
> And post o'er land and ocean without rest:
> They also serve who only stand and wait.

Work is also a gift because it's an opportunity to release human creativity, to bring something into existence that never existed before. Whether it's a new pen, keyboard, or spaghetti dish, or a superior design in a running shoe, or whatever it is, you created something that never existed before, and that is part of the expression of the divine nature: to create something new.

Furthermore, the Christian approach to work is that we do it unto the Lord. We're not looking to do it with eye service, as men pleasers, but to do the will of God from the soul. That's what Ephesians 6:6–8 teaches us. The Christian finds the hand of Christ in everything. When Jesus said, "I am with you always," that also means on the job.

Throughout the Bible, God dignified the value of work:

- God told Abraham to work: "Here is your land. Take care of it." This is a remarkable command—the first time in recorded history that God blessed and endorsed private property. He commanded Abraham, and all workers since then, to work their enterprise.
- He gave us work to accomplish during our earthly sojourn (Acts 13:2, 1 Cor. 16:10, Eph. 2:10).
- He appointed us over the works of his hands (Heb. 2:7).
- We are called to please God by bearing fruit in every good work (Col. 1:10, Heb. 13:21).
- Our work will be tested and examined by God (1 Cor. 3:13–15).

God commanded work for all peoples, for all generations, because:

- Work develops ability and builds character.
- Work, which is the prelude to earning money, allows us to care for ourselves and our families. See 1 Timothy 5:8 ("Anyone who does not provide for their relatives, and especially for their own household, has denied the faith and is worse than an unbeliever") and Ephesians 4:28 ("Anyone who has been stealing must steal no

longer, but must work, doing something useful with their own hands, that they may have something to share with those in need").

- Work enriches the world. Our contributions, expressed through work, enrich the lives of others. As Jim Stovall said, "In this life, work is the culmination of all we are. Work is the result of everything that we have learned, and that is a contribution we ultimately bring to others through the marketplace."[2]
- Our work and our workplace allow us to glorify God and feel fulfilled. Our work and workplace provide a context within which we can share Jesus Christ by doing our work with conscientious care, while building relationships with coworkers. This demonstrates character, conviction, and integrity.
- Work lifts depression. Read the plaque stamped on a prominent wall in Bellevue Hospital: "If you are depressed, work. If you're afraid, work. If you're feeling lazy, work. If you're hungry, work. If you're feeling useless and abandoned, work. Many of the world's ills and personal worries could be eliminated or prevented by people going out to work."

And listen to the challenge issued by Bob Vernon, former chief of police of the Los Angeles Police Department: "If you want to be a good *witness* for Jesus Christ on your job, then be the very best *worker* on your job."

Our American forefathers reminded us that our work not only brings glory to God but has immediate *moral* and *practical* benefits. They lived these scriptures:

For even when we were with you, we gave you this rule: "The one who is unwilling to work shall not eat." We hear that some among you are idle and disruptive. They are not busy; they are busybodies. Such people we command and urge in the Lord Jesus Christ to settle down and earn the food they eat. (2 Thess. 3:10–12)

Anyone who has been stealing must steal no longer, but must work, doing something useful with their own hands, that they may have something to share with those in need. (Eph. 4:28)

Richard Baxter, a Puritan leader, summed it up: "Be laborious and diligent in your calling . . . and if you cheerfully serve God in the labor of your hands with a heavenly and obedient mind, you will be as acceptable to him as if you had spent all that time in the more spiritual exercises of praying and kneeling."

Colonial leaders had to make statements like that, and live up to them, because colonial life was hard, hard, hard. Historian and author H. J. Sage writes:

Whether you were a colonist in New England, where winter blasts brought cold, sleet, and snow, or in the southern colonies, where oppressive heat and mosquitoes made the summers torturous, or anywhere in between, life was challenging . . . Everybody had to be productive for families to survive. Men and women, even in their separate spheres, had to work hard to support life. Conflicts with Indians could threaten life and limb, and on the edge of the frontier, other dangers lurked. These were hardy folk who risked everything to cross the ocean and embark on a new life, or they were descendants of those who had . . .

[T]hey believed in the notion that God helps those who help themselves . . . There was little room for slackers; as John Smith decreed in the Virginia colony, "He who does not work, will not eat."

. . . While the women had to sew, cook, take care of domestic animals, make many of the necessities used in the household such as soap, candles, clothing, and other necessities, the men were busy building, plowing, repairing tools, harvesting crops, hunting, fishing, and protecting the family from whatever threat might come . . .[3]

The work habits of those early settlers set the pattern for us today. Early in the twentieth century, German sociologist Max Weber wrote a book, *The Protestant Ethic and the Spirit of Capitalism*, that documented our indebtedness to our forefathers and their traditions and habits of work. We are all still benefitting from the patterns of this work ethic, which was praised by Jesus and dramatized by our forefathers.

Don't know about you, but I thank God every day that I was not born into a family of comfort. I strained and sweated for each skinny dime and each scarce greenback.

This is now my daily prayer of gratitude for the privilege of work and the joy of memory (go ahead and write your own):

Thank You, God, that at age five You gave me work.

Delivering groceries in my little red cart, earning twelve cents an hour from grocer Charlie Coco. Two hours. Twenty-four cents.

Big job, big deal.

Just enough change to see two Roy Rogers movies, a Superman serial, and a Looney Tunes cartoon. And, with a nickel tip from Mrs. Rich (God, You had a sense of humor to give her that name), I bought a Bit O Honey bar. And ate it. All by myself.

Thank You, Lord, that, at age eleven, I got work. Delivering Sunday papers. Five a.m., February in Boston. Walking the streets, nose as cold and hard as concrete, clouds of frost gushing from my mouth.

Thank You that, at age fifteen, I had the work of cleaning muck . . . those foot-high stacks of fertilizer dust that fell from the grinders. Crawling under those grinder belts and shoving aside mounds of manure mulch, I scooped up shovel after shovel. Every Saturday, getting it ready for the crew on Monday to mix and grind more manure and pellets.

Some called it crap.

I called it gold. Gave me money to help my welfare mom— and buy a bike.

Used and busted it was, but it rode like a flyer.

To me.

Work rescued us from worrying and got us off welfare. Thank you, Lord.

And in college . . .

"When the student is ready, the master will appear," and you did.

Tuition: a hundred dollars a semester. Remember, Lord? I didn't know there was a hundred dollars in the world. You showed up with work. Two jobs. During the week, Monday through Thursday, audiovisual library for the evening classes.

No calls? Slow night? Time for study.

And Friday through Saturday: medic work at the local hospital. No calls? Slow night? Time for study.

Why, some months I made two hundred dollars! Thank You again, Lord.

Paid my tuition, books, food, and clothes. And helped Mom.

Thank You, Lord, that after graduation You took me to Thailand with the Peace Corps. In the leper colonies, I learned a whole new side to work. Loving, serving, feeding, nursing, and learning how well off I really was.

Some had no toes, no eyes, no nose. Strips of cloth stuck to body parts for years. Ravaged by disease.

What an opportunity for unconditional love! Taking them to clinics for meds and surgery, finding clean homes for their children until they could be reunited with their disease-free parents. I learned that even the poorest welfare bums among us (like the Gallaghers) were Donald-Trump rich compared to most of the world.

And I learned that work and service to others go hand in hand.

Thank You, God, for work, that fire of self-esteem which enriches families and ignites progress, public and personal. In my work (really Your work), Lord, keep my focus intense and cheerful. Whether I'm:

cleaning commodes,

fixing teeth,

teaching a class,

clipping a hedge,

flipping a burger,

driving a truck,

running a company,

. . . or whatever,

I *will work with a passion for excellence, Lord, knowing by* Your *grace and power that all good work is honest and fulfilling.*

Work *is my daily devotion to* You, *and my daily gift to those dependent upon my work.*

This prayer, with its repetition of grateful memories, radiates (for me) a robust, healthy, and profitable view of work.

Work is not a necessary evil.

So we've seen that work is a gift. So is giving. And we've learned the importance of leveraging your money rather than loving or loathing it. Now we're going to look together at four different ways of earning money: as an employee, self-employed, business leader, or investor. These four categories apply to virtually every worker at some point in his or her life, and you will notice that it's quite possible that at some point, you have been in each of these categories—or will be.

The principles in each of these sections apply to everyone, not only those within that category. You may not be an owner or manager, but you are likely a leader in some other area of your life—your home, church, sports team, class, club, or council. You may not be self-employed, but you would do well to utilize the same strategies to accomplish your most treasured goals. You have financial resources that you should desire to maintain and grow even if you have never considered yourself an investor.

We are all workers. God designed us this way.

Notes

1. Bruce Alferd, "Why Work?" *Christianity Today*, July 14, 1989, 38.
2. Jim Stovall, *The Ultimate Gift* (David Cook, 2007), 15.
3. Sage American History, accessed December 3, 2014, www .sageamericanhistory.net.

Jesus on Money

How to Earn It

Employee

Let's consider the first of the four categories: earning money by working as an employee, Jesus Style.

In the movie *Courageous,* there is a wonderful Christ-like model of an employee. I'll summarize the scene. It goes something like this:

Consolidated Company (CC) President rules the plant from a desk the size of a ping-pong table. To his right sits the CFO, arms folded and face taut. They summon an employee named Javier, tell him to sit, and explain how pleased they are with his work. They want to make him a manager in the warehouse, raising his salary $500 a month with no more nightshifts or weekends. There's only one catch: they want to know he's loyal to the company.

"I love this company," Javier says.

"You'll be counting inventory," Prez says, picking up the tempo. "Keeping track of boxes of supplies as equipment comes in, among other things. Very easy, but very important."

"Of course. Of course."

". . . and the fewer boxes we receive, that means we have fewer supplies with which to work. On paper. We can show our shareholders and stock owners that with relatively few supplies, we produce quality and quantity products. Looks good for everyone. Makes more money for everyone, including managers like you, Javier. Are you with me?"

"I think so."

"So . . ." CFO leans forward from his gunmetal, padded folding chair. "When the boxes come in, you count only half of them."

"Half?"

"Yes," CFO continues, "if a pallet has sixteen boxes, you count eight. If it has fifty boxes, you write down twenty-five. That's what you write down. Do you follow me?"

"That's, uh, not exactly telling the truth. Is that what you're saying?" Javier timidly asks.

"We're saying," Prez emphasizes, "we want to know if you're a loyal member of the team, if you're committed, really committed to helping this company grow. Can we count on you?"

Javier leans forward, staring at a dead mosquito on the checkered tile beneath him. "I have to talk to my wife. I have to think about it."

"Of course," Prez says. "You go home, talk to your wife, and we'll meet here at ten tomorrow."

At home, Javier tells his wife, Juanita, the good news and the bad news. They swat the choices back and forth like a tennis ball. They are behind on rent, they need the health benefits—their children need their shots—and they worry that Javier may be fired completely if he does not agree. Without a job, they don't know how they will get food, make the car payments, keep the lights on. Their kids join them, and together they pray.

"God, help me," Javier prays. "God, help us."

At five minutes till ten the next morning, Javier takes the longest walk he's ever taken in his life. Past the assembly line and past lines of shipping/receiving tables, he walks to the office of the Prez. Prez and CFO get right to the point and ask for his decision. Is he on the team or not?

Javier tells them, "I am very grateful for my job and want to keep it, and I'm very grateful for the chance to be a manager . . . but I cannot lie like you're asking me to do. I feel it would dishonor my God and my family and would not be right for this company, either."

"Is that your final decision?" Prez asks.

"Yes."

Javier's head is down. He hears their chairs scrape against the floor and then sees their shoes in front of him. Both men stand there with hands outstretched.

CFO says, "Javier, I want to shake the hand of a man with integrity."

Prez adds, "We have interviewed five people, Javier, and you are the first one to stand firm on doing what's right. Congratulations on your new position as the manager of the Shipping and Receiving Department."

Minutes later, Javier calls his wife, waiting desperately by the phone. "It was a test, a *test*, honey."

In her kitchen, Juanita is jumping, laughing, crying, screaming, "Thank you, God, thank you."

Trust: The foundation of service in life, the foundation of service as an employee. This scene is a profound example of integrity, which is itself a manifestation of courage. Remember this: courage is the very foundation of integrity. Both business owners and God are looking for people with this type of courage. Jesus said in Luke 16:10, "Whoever can be trusted with very little can also be trusted with much, and whoever is dishonest with very little will also be dishonest with much."

Javier's story shows not only Jesus's principle of trust, but Jesus's principle of the Golden Rule, "Do unto others as you would have them do unto you."

As an employee, you ask yourself:

- If this were my company, how would I want my employees to act?
- How important would it be to make sure my employees were trustworthy?
- Do I walk off with company postage or stationery?
- Do I bang out dozens of personal copies on company machines?
- Do I speak honorably of the company?
- When I have an issue with a fellow worker or boss, do I go directly to him or her?
- Do I "cyber-loaf" using company time to surf the Internet?
- Do I gossip? Am I jealous of fellow employees?

Jesus tells a story exposing this self-centered attitude:

> For the kingdom of heaven is like a landowner who went out early in the morning to hire workers for his vineyard. He agreed to pay them a denarius for the day and sent them into his vineyard.
>
> About nine in the morning he went out and saw others standing in the marketplace doing nothing. He told them, "You also go and work in my vineyard, and I will pay you whatever is right." So they went.
>
> He went out again about noon and about three in the afternoon and did the same thing. About five in the afternoon he went out and found still others standing around. He asked them, "Why have you been standing here all day long doing nothing?"
>
> "Because no one has hired us," they answered.
>
> He said to them, "You also go and work in my vineyard."
>
> When evening came, the owner of the vineyard said to his foreman, "Call the workers and pay them their wages, beginning with the last ones hired and going on to the first."
>
> The workers who were hired about five in the afternoon came and each received a denarius. So when those came who were hired first, they expected to receive more. But each one of them also received a denarius. When they received it, they began to grumble against the landowner. "These who were hired last worked only one hour," they

said, "and you have made them equal to us who have borne the burden of the work and the heat of the day."

But he answered one of them, "I am not being unfair to you, friend. Didn't you agree to work for a denarius? Take your pay and go. I want to give the one who was hired last the same as I gave you. Don't I have the right to do what I want with my own money? Or are you envious because I am generous?" (Matt. 20: 1–15)

Ask yourself:

- Do I clock in/clock out accurately?
- Do I pad expense accounts? Do I embezzle?
- Do I thank God every day for my job and ask him to show me how to anticipate the needs of my boss, coworkers, and customers?
- When appropriate, do I thank my boss without sounding like I am "sucking up"?
- Do I work *"unto the Lord"*?

"Whatever you do, work at it with all your heart, as working for the Lord, not for human masters . . ." (Col. 3:23).

Javier's bosses saw in him the principle of "work unto the Lord."

Whether it is fixing a computer, delivering packages, stuffing burritos, repairing a tire, or writing a multimillion-dollar budget, do your bosses see an attitude of excellence and trustworthiness that transcends merely earning a paycheck?

The issue of earning money as an employee was addressed in Luke 16:12: "Whoever can be trusted with very little can be trusted with very much." As employees, we embrace our responsibilities, no matter how big or how small, as if we own the company. We take intense pride in the final product or service. We have a passion for excellence no matter how little the job appears to be.

Consider John 13:6–7: "Simon Peter said to him, 'Lord, are you going to wash my feet?' Jesus replied, 'You do not realize now what I am doing, but later you will understand.'"

The attitude of a Christ-like employee *is* the attitude of a servant. Before you progress into becoming a self-employed person, or a business leader, or a prudent investor, you learn first to serve.

The really good news is that the attitudes of *trustworthiness, faithfulness,* and *service* allow the worker/leader/investor to enjoy the kingdom of God right now. Enjoying the kingdom of God right now means the rule of God's love is in your heart this minute. You express that love by appreciating the opportunity to have a job in America and showing it through your words and work.

Donald Trump sums it up nicely: "When you're an employee, always pretend that you're working for yourself. Always pretend that you own the company."

2

Jesus on Money

2a. Don't Love It

2b. Do Give It

Part One: The Gift of Giving

Part Two: Are You a Flint, Sponge, or Honeycomb?

2c. How to Earn It

Part One: Employee

Part Two: Self-Employed

Part Three: Business Leader: The Boss

2d. How to Make It Grow: Power, Profit, Peace of Mind, and Putting People First

Part One: Jesus on Growing Money

Part Two: Jesus's Talent Parable

Part Three: Jesus's Tower Parable

Part Four: The Tower Parable and the Power of Critical Reasoning

Part Five: Jesus's Mustard Seed Parable: Let My Money Grow

Part Six: Jesus on Taxes

How to Earn It

Self-Employed

Esteemed neurosurgeon and 2016 presidential candidate Dr. Ben Carson said, "No risk, pay the cost. Know risk, reap the rewards."

He's talking about the self-employed.

Goals

You're on your own.

And you better have a goal.

Jesus did.

"As the time approached for him to be taken up to heaven, Jesus *resolutely* set out for Jerusalem" (Luke 9:51, my emphasis).

Jesus set his face toward Jerusalem. Jesus had a clear and compelling goal.

Over the years, I have interviewed Dr. Charles Stanley, Joel Osteen, Johnny Bench, Nolan Ryan, Ann Coulter,

Michael Medved, Zig Ziglar, Governor Mike Huckabee, Dr. Ken Cooper, and many others. Now, I have never had an interview with the legendary Michael Jordan, but let's imagine for a minute that I did and how that could have gone.

Let's suppose I grabbed the basketball megastar for an interview when the Bulls were in town to play the Mavericks, and then I asked if we could play one on one after the game so I could tell my children and grandchildren that I played against Michael Jordan.

There we were: legendary Michael Jordan and not so legendary W. Neil Gallagher, college basketball player of the '60s, now writer, radio host, and financial counselor.

I beat Michael 28–4 in our ten-minute drill.

The reason I beat Michael Jordan is that I blindfolded him.

Can you picture that happening? Neither can I. Would Michael Jordan play blindfolded? *Would he shoot at a goal that he could not see?*

How about you?

You don't stumble into your self-employed venture every day because that's what you did yesterday. You don't produce your product or service hour by hour just because that's what you did the hour before. You are self-employed. Your choice. That means (at first) you are the janitor, president, secretary, bookkeeper, plumber, dispatcher, and receptionist.

You took the risk that Jesus commended: "For whoever has, and uses it, will be given more, and they will have an abundance. Whoever does not have, even what they have will be taken from them. And throw that worthless servant outside, into the darkness, where there will be weeping and gnashing of teeth" (Matt. 25:29–30).

You're on your own. No sick pay. No paid vacation. No company benefits.

"You do not work, you do not eat."

You personify the truth that Mark Hansen, co-creator of the *Chicken Soup for the Soul* series, stated: "To get great rewards in life, you have to take great and calculated risks, in order to realize, energize, and fully potential-ize your value to yourself, your life, your future, and the marketplace."

For the people who work with you, "They do not work, they do not eat." They know the risk. They believe in you.

You make it clear to yourself and others:

1. This is about service.
2. This is about production.
3. This is about results.

To accomplish this, you must see your goals. Glue your eyeballs to them. Ignite the engine called your brain to race after your goals straight and fast, because *goals fire up the imagination and give you the power to keep going.*

Grab a 5x7 card, and write your goal or goals on it. Slip it in your pocket, and recite daily, especially at those two critical times: at night, when your message of power soaks into your subconscious, and first thing in the morning to get your day roaring.

By the grace and power of God, this is my goal:

_____

_____

I know I have the ability to achieve this goal. Therefore, I act on an hourly and daily basis to achieve the goal. I understand the thoughts in my mind will reproduce themselves into outward physical actions. Therefore, I dedicate this goal throughout the day to God, his power, the service of others, and the enrichment and expansion of my skills.

I create in my mind a clear mental picture. I realize the truth that the ultimate victory is not always to the swift, but to those who keep on running. I keep on running toward the goal, and I succeed by attracting to myself the cooperation of others. I inspire others to help me because of my willingness to help them. I understand that in pursuit of my goal, I know I am attacked by forces both within and without.

Within, I am attacked by fear, laziness, and discouragement. I repeat Jesus's command, "Satan, get behind me and leave me alone."

Without, I am attacked by competitors and envious people who want to see me fail. I remind myself of the truth that all those who desire to live godly in Christ Jesus are persecuted.

In pursuit of my goal, I act with passion.

I am assaulted by fear and anger, but I do not let them control me. I eliminate envy, hatred, and selfishness by developing love for all humanity because I know a negative attitude toward others can never bring me success. I cause others to believe in me because I believe in them and in myself. I sign my name to this card and commit it to memory and repeat it out loud often with full faith that it directs my actions so that I fulfill my goals, energized by the power of God and the passion to serve others.

You've written your own goals statement, and you read it often, because you know: *people who do not have goals are controlled by those who do.*

Didn't write your goals?

Drop the book.

Fugeddabout it!

You're not serious.

Don't go forward until you write your goals.

You're back. You have written your goals. You've embraced the adventure, and you're willing to take the risks associated with fighting for your goals. Your eyes are open, your heart is full, your will is strong, and you shout your power statement: "I will make today a great day, fulfilling my goals regardless of what other people say, think, or do."

Early Rising

You're self-employed. You're a courageous entrepreneur (CE). And you are the leader of your own 5:00 a.m. club.

Mary Kay Ash of the legendary Mary Kay Cosmetics inspired her associates to join *her* 5:00 a.m. club.

5:00 a.m. Get an hour or two jump on everyone else.

No late-night TV. No late-night dinners.

Ash and her associates practiced Benjamin Franklin's classic statement "Early to bed and early to rise makes a man [or a woman] healthy, wealthy, and wise."

Jesus commended the practice of rising early:

For the kingdom of heaven is like a landowner who went out early in the morning to hire workers for his vineyard. He agreed to pay them a denarius for the day and sent them into his vineyard. (Matt. 20:1–2)

. . . but Jesus went to the Mount of Olives. At dawn he appeared again in the temple courts, where all the people gathered around him, and he sat down to teach them. (John 8:1–2)

When you rise, slap your feet on the floor and shout, "I'm alive, and I'm awake; I am up, and I feel great. I feel good, I feel fine, I feel this way all the time. Champions serve, champions soar, champions give, more, more, more. And I am a champion."

Sound silly? Feel like saying it?

Not as silly as d-r-a-g-g-i-n-g through a morning or entire day like sloshing through mud and drowning yourself with feelings of doubt and fear.

Say it again. "I'm alive, and I'm awake; I am up, and I feel great. I feel good, I feel fine, I feel this way all the time. Champions serve, champions soar, champions give, more, more, more. And I am a champion."

Sheila Walsh, in her book *We Brake for Joy*, says: "Whatever you are going through at the moment, remember this is not the end of your story. We are morning people called to live by faith and not by sight. To lift our hearts to God in the darkness because we have the promise of the morning."[1]

The Psalmist said, "It may be dark at night, but joy comes in the morning" (Psalm 30:5).

Grab the day early. Proclaim the morning a miracle of joy and power.

Read those goals upon arising. They are smack in front of you on the refrigerator, computer, dashboard, and bathroom mirror. You are allowing them to burn deep into your subconscious.

Affirmations

Add to your goals these affirmations:

My Affirmations & The Laws of Progress

- Unexpected help comes from unpredictable sources to those who remain positive, enthusiastic, and cheerful.
- No one knows enough to worry.
- Two kinds of people: those who blame God for what they do not have, and those who thank God for what they do have.
- You change who you are, what you are, and where you are by changing what goes into your mind.
- Self-pity is a luxury that leaders cannot afford.
- What you've got and where you are is plenty good enough to build again.
- You will move ever forward and upward by following the Law of Persistence, the Law of Action, and the Law of Progress.

Unexpected help comes from unpredictable sources to those who remain positive, enthusiastic, and cheerful.

In the midst of disaster and heartache, it's hard enough just to press on, much less to "feel good" and be enthusiastic and cheerful. The last thing you feel like doing is radiating goodwill and optimism to others. You're in a dark mood, and you want to take out your fears, frustration, and resentment on those who (you think) deserve it and even those who don't.

Like a laser, focus on the good, on the blessings you have received, and the opportunities ahead. Whatever comes your way, stay positive, and something amazing will happen—you will find out that you are not alone.

There are people out there who believe in you and will help you. You just don't know who they are yet, or when they will appear. They will find you, and you will find them. You will attract to yourself those forces and those persons who will help you achieve your goals.

No one knows enough to worry.

When we worry, we choose to negatively project our brains into the future, moaning and complaining like a calf lost in a blizzard crying for its mama.

> "I know the next five minutes will be bad,
> or the next five months,
> or the next five years."
> "It'll never work out."
> "I give up."
> "This is it. I'm done!"
> Danger.

No hope.

The end of life.

We can live forty days without food, four days without water, four minutes without air, but only four seconds without hope.

In our human understanding, we perceive such a tiny fraction of the big picture that it's both pointless and destructive to act as if we understand the grand design. It's like peering through a drinking straw at one square centimeter of the Sistine Chapel and complaining that the colors are off and the image makes no sense. We have no perspective. Bust the worry, smash the despair, early and quick.

No one knows enough to worry.

Two kinds of people: those who blame God for what they do not have, and those who thank God for what they do have.

When we complain, we get more of what we complain about. When we give thanks, we get more of what we're giving thanks for. It's a choice.

Gratitude releases blessings from the hand of God and the hands of others, like a fire hydrant uncorked by a firefighter releases a torrent of water.

Without the perspective of gratitude, a person looks backward with shame and looks forward with fear. *With* the perspective of gratitude, a person looks inward, now in the present, to seize a power called free will, igniting a desire to move forward and succeed.

There are two kinds of people. Make a point to be the thankful kind.

You change who you are, what you are, and where you are by changing what goes into your mind.

The Indian chief was telling stories to his grandson: "My son, there are two wolves in you. One is mean, vicious, angry, hateful. The other wolf in you is kind, cheerful, helpful, generous. These wolves in you fight for your spirit."

"Grandpa, which wolf wins?"

"Whichever one you feed."

Be selective and guarded: feed your mind only with what is pure, positive, and powerful (P-P-P). Radio, TV, movies, phone, Internet, Facebook, books, conversations . . . stuff the cavities of your brain only with the type of P-P-P food that will empower you to change yourself and your circumstances into something greater.

Seize this motto: "P-P-P or it's not for me!"

Self-pity is a luxury that leaders (like you) do not embrace.
The reason (among others) that you do not embrace self-pity is because . . . *people need you.*

You know that your life is a stone dropped in the middle of a lake. The great concentric circles that eventually blanket the lake and touch the shores illustrate how you touch people, now and later. Many of your influential touches you'll never know about.

People need to see you persist. People need your courage and leadership. You're not selfish; you're strong. You're not timid; you're tough. You don't surrender to self-pity. Period. You just don't.

What you've got and where you are is plenty good enough to build again.

You may feel that you don't have what you need to start over, to build afresh. You've made mistakes; maybe your financial tower has collapsed, maybe your castle in the sky has crumbled. The foundation that remains doesn't look too promising.

Here's the good news: God specializes in fresh starts.

Look at Job—he lost his children, his wealth, his property, and his health. God restored what he had lost and doubled his original riches.

Or consider Moses, the stammering, stuttering murderer living in shame and exile from his people. Fast forward and God is using him to part the Red Sea and lead his people to the Promised Land.

What about Joseph, thrown into a well by his own brothers, sold into slavery, then unjustly accused and tossed into jail? God saw a foundation of faith and integrity, and he built on it until Joseph was placed in charge of all Egypt, second only to the Pharaoh.

Paul could attest. He was struck blind on the road to Damascus after years of persecuting Christians. One encounter with Jesus and a new house was built—you might call it a temple for the Holy Spirit. Paul wrote half the New Testament and arguably did more to spread the Gospel throughout the world than any Christian in history.

You get the idea.

What you've got and where you are is plenty good enough to build again.

The Law of Persistence

You can't see the future any more than you can see all the road at night. But you don't have to see all the road ahead of you. Keep driving. One hundred feet at a time.

You don't know where the next bend is. That's OK. All you need is one hundred feet of light illuminating what's in front of you. You just keep driving with a positive, enthusiastic, and cheerful attitude.

You haven't grabbed your goal yet, and you can't see all the obstacles, but you keep going.

You keep driving,

And driving,

And driving.

The Law of Action

True, we do not know the next five minutes, or the next five months, or the next five years. What we do know is that we cannot predict the future, but we do create it by our moment-to-moment actions.

Action, action, action.

Act. Move. Talk. Run. Walk. Write . . . Go. Go. Go. Keep moving forward. Bust out of bed; put ice cubes on your eyes. Step outside, suck in five deep breaths, return to the house, and take a cold shower.

You will feel good sharing your valuable product or services today. And your customers, clients, patients, students, or readers will feel so good enjoying the benefits of your product or service. They need you.

You embrace this truth: When you do what you love, people will love what you do.

Millions wait until they feel good before they act in positive ways, but the self-employed leaders (like you) *act* in positive ways, and the feelings follow. And so do the solutions and successes.

The Law of Progress

Yard by yard, anything seems hard, but inch by inch, anything's a cinch. When problems threaten to crush you, and when Satan screams in your skull, "There is no hope, and there are no solutions," here's what you do:

> Say it out loud: "Satan, by the power and the name of Jesus Christ, leave me alone."
> Shout your goals.
> Do the next thing right,
> and the next thing,
> and the next thing.

If the next thing means pouring a glass of water, do it slowly and successfully. Hold it steady, let the water run until it gets cool, pour half a glass so it doesn't spill. Drink it slowly.

Good, you accomplished that job.

Now rinse the glass, dry it off, put it in the cabinet.

Good. You're a person of order and control.

Your next job is to wipe off the sink. Good. You wiped it off. It looks clean. Good job.

Now you sit at your desk or table and write your victory.

Write about the fires of worry raging in your skull. Write it, write it, write it.

At first, it will feel like shoving your hand in a fire. It'll hurt. But the fire will fade and your healing will come. Here's how you do it.

Two columns:

On the left-hand side, write the list of your fears and worries. On the right-hand side, write the actions you will take now.

Keep writing. The creative juices will flow to show you solutions. This exercise is therapeutic, practical, and, in some cases, life saving.

After writing, speak. Call someone. A child, a spouse, a coworker. Call someone—anyone—just to talk.

Ask them, "How can I help you?" You do this because you know:

a. Everyone is having a tough day, and everyone needs help in some way.
b. The best way to help yourself is to help others. Depressed? Lift someone else up, and you won't feel depressed. Feeling lonely? Befriend another, and you won't feel lonely.

Good. That's done. You know how to punch a cell phone, and you know how to talk to people and help them.

Slow and deliberate . . . you build up your self-confidence. You're learning that inch by inch, anything's a cinch.

Keep it up.

Do the next thing right, and the next thing, and the next thing.

Love and Need

You are chasing after your goals, step by step. You are reading your affirmations daily and committing them to memory. You are following the Laws of Progress.

Now the test of the self-employed, courageous entrepreneur is this: "I would provide my goods and services to you, my client, customer, or friend, *even if I were not getting paid*, because these goods or services are good *for you*. I want you to have them. The profit I make from them, both emotional and financial, is a serendipity."

In providing goods and services, shoot for the top. Pay yourself the full value of what you're worth. You would recommend that to others, wouldn't you? Recommend it to yourself. People will not value you any more than you value yourself.

> I bargained with life for a penny only to learn, dismayed
> That any wage I would have asked of life, life would have paid.[2]

You work with a passion. You combine pride in your product or service with love for people. You deserve to be paid with a profit. And enjoy the truth Robert Frost penned so well:

> But yield who will to their separation,
> My object in living is to unite

My avocation and my vocation
As my two eyes make one in sight.
Only where love and need are one,
And the work is play for mortal stakes,
Is the deed ever really done
For Heaven and the future's sakes.[3]

God put your skill in your heart, so put your heart into your work. That's where *your* love and need are one.

And when you combine your love of work with love for others, they will say of you what they said of S. Truett Cathy: "Truett Cathy is living proof that you can own and run a business on Christian principles and make it through this world of greed and deception. Cathy built his life and business based on hard work, humility, and biblical principles."[4] Based on these principles, all of Chick-fil-A's restaurants operate with a "Closed on Sunday" policy, without exception.

What exactly did Truett Cathy's work ethic produce?

His WinShape Homes program to help children is but one example of how this man has used his life, his wealth, and his love to help others.

"As part of his WinShape Homes® program, nine foster care homes have been established in Georgia, two in Tennessee, and one in Alabama that are operated by Cathy and the WinShape Foundation. These homes, accommodating up to 12 children with two fulltime foster parents, provide long-term care for foster children with a positive family environment."[5]

Thank you, Lord. Thank you, Truett Cathy.

Truett Cathy's wealth never changed him from the humble, dedicated person that he always was. One of his favorite Bible verses was Proverbs 22:11: "A good name is rather to be chosen than great riches."

Notes

1. Sheila Walsh, et. al., *We Brake For Joy* (Zondervan, 1998).
2. Laurie Beth Jones, *Jesus, CEO* (New York: Hyperion Books, 1995), 3.
3. Robert Frost, "Two Tramps in Mud Time," *North of Boston: Poems* (New York: Dodd and Company, 1977).
4. "Church Announces Grave Condition of S. Truett Cathy, Founder of Chick-fil-A," September 7, 2014, www.examiner.com.
5. "S. Truett Cathy: 2013 Georgia Trustee," Georgia Historical Society, www.georgiahistory.com.

Jesus on Money

2a. Don't Love It

2b. Do Give It

Part One: The Gift of Giving

Part Two: Are You a Flint, Sponge, or Honeycomb?

2c. How to Earn It

Part One: Employee

Part Two: Self-Employed

Part Three: Business Leader: The Boss

2d. How to Make It Grow: Power, Profit, Peace of Mind, and Putting People First

Part One: Jesus on Growing Money

Part Two: Jesus's Talent Parable

Part Three: Jesus's Tower Parable

Part Four: The Tower Parable and the Power of Critical Reasoning

Part Five: Jesus's Mustard Seed Parable: Let My Money Grow

Part Six: Jesus on Taxes

How to Earn It

Business Leader (BL): The Boss

The third way to earn money: as a business leader.

Two types: owner and manager.

Owner: You bought, inherited, or started a business. You're the owner, and everyone works for you and the company.

Manager: You work for the owner of the company. You're not "just an employee." You hire, fire, train, manage, and supervise. You make money for the company, and you train others to make money for the company.

Your title is vice president, team leader, supervisor, director, manager, CEO, CFO, or . . . whatever.

You are responsible to the owner and to the company for leading and motivating employees to produce goods and services, serve customers, make a profit, and earn money for you, the company, and employees. All the principles of a business leader described below apply whether you are owner or manager.

Owner or manager, you want a mission statement. Jesus made his mission clear:

"The Son of Man came to seek and save the lost."

His followers didn't get it at first. But, by his words and work, Jesus made his mission statement clear. Then and now.

As a BL, you're a leader of the company mission, and you're smacked with the same temptations that have smacked leaders for centuries, including Jesus himself: hunger, power, and greed.

> Then Jesus was led by the Spirit into the wilderness to be tempted by the devil. After fasting forty days and forty nights, he was hungry. The tempter came to him and said, "If you are the Son of God, tell these stones to become bread."
>
> Jesus answered, "It is written: 'Man shall not live on bread alone, but on every word that comes from the mouth of God.'"
>
> Then the devil took him to the holy city and had him stand on the highest point of the temple. "If you are the Son of God," he said, "throw yourself down. For it is written: 'He will command his angels concerning you, and they will lift you up in their hands, so that you will not strike your foot against a stone.'"
>
> Jesus answered him, "It is also written: 'Do not put the Lord your God to the test.'"
>
> Again, the devil took him to a very high mountain and showed him all the kingdoms of the

world and their splendor. "All this I will give you," he said, "if you will bow down and worship me."

—Matthew 4:1–9

Hunger. "If you are the son of God, tell these stones to become bread." Jesus hungered for immediate gratification. In this case, for food. Eating would have smashed his mission, poisoned his integrity, and stunted his progress.

Still true today.

When a BL surrenders to immediate gratification, short-term profits, and self-indulgent pleasure, he smashes his mission, poisons his integrity, and stunts his progress.

You're the BL, and when you are hit with the temptation for immediate gratification (and you will be), or quick and questionable profits, it's imperative that you scream at Satan like Jesus did: "Satan, get behind me. Leave me alone."

In brief, Jesus told Satan that man does not live to gratify the flesh, meaning a BL does not surrender to short-term and selfish pleasures.

Jesus said it hard and tight: "Man does not live on bread alone."

A business leader following the model of Jesus does not live on profits or pleasure alone but truly on every word that comes from the mouth of God. And those words are always packed with love, meaning the BL trains himself or herself and trains others to pursue actions that are in the best interest of others.

That's self-control. That's integrity. That's smart, and eventually very profitable for everyone . . . because what goes around, comes around.

> **Power.** "Throw yourself down and command your angels that they will lift you up and you will not strike your foot against a stone."

Here, Satan tempts Jesus to display his power. In today's culture, Satan would offer him the symbols of power: Rolex toys, a corner office, a limousine with chauffeur, a university named in his honor, and a mansion in the Hamptons.

To attack this temptation for power, the BL harnesses an attitude of meekness.

Like Jesus.

Only two people in the Bible are called meek, Moses and Jesus. Meekness is strength *under control*. It channels power into positive purposes.

"Power corrupts and absolute power corrupts absolutely," said Lord Acton. Meekness, on the other hand, channels the power urges of a BL to provide a model of service that is productive, compassionate, and profitable for all.

> **Greed.** "All this I will give you if you bow down and worship me," Satan announced to Jesus while pointing to the kingdoms of the world.

Greed is to profit what lust is to sex. Sex is a good and healthy impulse, seeking ultimate fulfillment in a commitment between a man and a woman called marriage, within which the ecstasy of sexual love unfolds.

Lust is the abuse of sex.

Profit is a good and healthy motive, seeking ultimate fulfillment in serving others with goods or services. This is the dictum of Adam Smith, talking about the invisible hand meeting the needs of others while meeting your own needs. Zig Ziglar summarized it: "You can have everything in life you want if you will just help enough other people get what they want."

Greed is the abuse of profit. Greed is using people through whatever means are expedient: cheating, stealing, lying. People who give in to greed are people who believe Satan's lies and surrender to his leadership. Essentially, they bow to Satan and worship him by their immoral actions.

The BL recoils from these temptations and vigorously works to empower team members and employees with the profit attitudes of service and significance. He or she enlists their talents and skills for the joint objectives of making a profit for all and does not exploit them with a motive of greed.

But I've got to make a lot of money in order to lead my employees. That's what they want.

The prevailing business paradigm would have us believe that what employees want most is more money and more time off.

"Shatter this dangerous paradigm," says Daniel H. Pink in his magnificent book *Drive*. His surveys document that what employees want most is respect, freedom, flexibility, purpose, and significance.

They want trust invested in them rather than money thrown at them.

In my radio interview with Robert Kiyosaki, best-selling author of books such as *Rich Dad, Poor Dad*, he summarized this truth by saying that the way to build success for yourself is to build a relationship with other people based upon trust and service while achieving your goals.

Employees want to use heart, mind, body, and soul in unleashing their skills in a productive work effort, serving *others*. That's dignity and significance.

Hunger, power, and greed are streams of energy turned inward, with a self-serving passion: "For me!" "For me!" "For me!"

BLs turn their streams of energy outward. For others. BLs want employees and customers to feel important and special, dramatized by Jesus's example of servant-leadership at the Lord's Supper.

Do you remember his example? He washed their feet, dramatizing the leadership principle "I'm the leader and that means I am here to serve you."

1. *BLs give team members the freedom to fail and learn from their mistakes.* Consider the three-year training that Jesus gave Peter, knowing that at one point Peter would fail—falling flat on his face in denying his Lord. In spite of this, Jesus trusted Peter and knew Peter would learn from his mistakes.

In the early days of IBM, a trusted employee came to Thomas J. Watson Sr., an IBM CEO and later board chairman, and said, "Mr. Watson, I am submitting my resignation. I made a mistake today that is going to cost this company $1 million." Watson replied, "You are not going anywhere. Why would I let you go when it just cost me $1 million to teach you a lesson?" Employees and team members need to feel free to fail. They need the adventure of risk. They need to know that their BL trusts them enough to grow, challenge, and experiment.

2. BLs give team members the opportunity to ask, to doubt, to question. Jesus gave this opportunity to his followers as they trekked through the desert and questioned his many meetings with mad men, a Samaritan woman, and angry Pharisees. The epitome of this approach came with Thomas and his insistence on seeing Jesus's hands and feet: "Unless I see the nail marks in his hands and put my finger where the nails were, and put my hand into his side, I will not believe" (John 20:25).

Let 'em doubt and ask. Eventually, they will see and follow, as Thomas eventually did with Jesus.

3. BLs understand that team members want to be free to complete a statement like this: "If I had the freedom to fail, I would (_fill in the blank_) to help make this company better" and "I can best contribute by (_fill in the blank_)."

4. BLs understand the threat of ego. BLs do not let their egos interfere. BLs understand the severity of the following question: "Do I want to succeed, or do I want to have my own way?" Unsuccessful leaders think those are the same things. They think having their own way and succeeding are one.

They are not!

Savvy BLs keep the *goal* of success in mind. Keep your goals burning, visible, and hot. With each temptation, ask the question "Do I want to win an argument to prove I am right? Or do I want to succeed overall?"

Smash the ego. Fire up the goal.

5. BLs understand team members do not want to be treated as objects of profit. They want to be treated as persons of unconditional worth.

6. BLs understand the value of experience. They understand older employees (now that's a flexible term that can refer to anyone over forty in today's marketplace) are wondering, "Is the boss going to dump me for someone he can get for half the price straight out of high school or college?" BLs let their team members relax as they emphasize that business leaders value experience and reward it.

7. BLs catch team members doing what's right. MBWA: Management By Wandering Around. They look for people doing right, praise them, and publicly reward them. BLs practice Emperor Napoleon's truth: "People will die for a ribbon."

8. BLs give team members the tools they need, the training on how to use those tools, and the freedom to succeed . . . and then they let go.

9. BLs place the company's mission statement in prominent places: computers, mirrors, locker rooms, break rooms, etc.

Our mission statement at Gallagher Financial Group, Inc.: *To be a vehicle of God's profit, peace, comfort, and power to as many people as possible, helping first with their financial success and also with their spiritual, emotional, and family well-being.*

Clients know, and team members know, that in our company *people are more important than profits* and *relationships are more important than revenue.* We keep this truth in front of us.

10. BLs correct in private and praise in public.

11. BLs let people on the front line make the decisions. It is precisely because they are on the front line that team members who are in direct contact with customers, vendors, and the marketplace can execute the best decisions.

12. BLs practice the principle of delegation, following the example of Moses in Exodus 18:17–23:

> Moses's father-in-law Jethro said to Moses: "Why are you trying to do this all alone? There are people standing here all day long to help. It's not right," his father-in-law explained. "You're going to wear yourself out, and if you do, what will happen to the people? Moses, don't try to handle all this by yourself. Now listen, let me give you a word of advice and God will bless you. Be the people's representative, bringing to him the question to decide. You tell them his decisions, teaching them God's laws, and showing them the principle of God in living. Find some faithful, godly, honest men and appoint them as judges. One judge for each one thousand people,

and he in turn will appoint judges under him, each in charge of a hundred. And then each of them will appoint two judges, each responsible for fifty people. Each of them will have five judges beneath him, each for every ten persons. Let these men be responsible to serve people with justice at all times. Everything that is too important or complicated will fall to you, but the smaller matters are taken care of themselves. It will be easier for you, because you will share the burden with them. If you follow this advice, there will be peace and harmony in the camp."

BLs also follow the example of Jesus as he dispatched his disciples to get ready for the next meeting: "Jesus made the disciples get into the boat and go *prepare* ahead of him on the other side, while he dismissed the crowd" (Matt. 14:22, my emphasis).

13. BLs give team members opportunities to grow through academic training, attitude enhancement, and on-the-job skill training.

A classic example of business leadership on a grand scale is the company Panda Express and its two leaders, Andrew and Peggy Cherng. I heard about the Cherngs from Robert Kiyosaki during an interview. Like me, they are big fans of the biblical principles for leaders and success taught by Stephen Covey in his book *The 7 Habits of Highly Effective People.*

Enjoy with me the habits of planning, vision, hard work, customer service, and employee recognition dramatized by the Cherngs and their amazing enterprise called Panda Express:

1. The Cherngs acknowledge that Panda Express is (of course) Chinese fast food, and it's hard to eat Chinese food while driving.

2. So . . . the Cherngs emphasize that Panda is *not* about Chinese food or even fast food. Panda is about giving a maximum enjoyable experience to customers and providing an enjoyable atmosphere for team members. The Cherngs took a "negative" (i.e., fast food) and turned it into a positive: superior customer service.

3. Feeling the Cherngs' passion for enjoyment and excellence, customers are glad to come back, and team members are glad to learn, grow, and support Panda.

For example, Andrew Cherng cites the story of an uneducated Hispanic man who started out washing dishes and spoke no English. They brought him up through the ranks, and, today, he is one of their most productive regional chefs. The man's daughter is in the honors program at school.

"Panda," the Cherngs insist, "is all about team members who are growing professionally and personally."

4. The Cherngs teach that working with your head and having great textbook skills are important, but it's much more important to learn how to work with your heart—that is, with a passion for excellence.

In that pursuit, the Cherngs require that any prospective employee read Stephen Covey's *The 7 Habits of Highly Effective People* first and discuss it with the Cherngs before being hired. Panda assumes every team member will make a habit of excelling in everything they do. In their view, you excel in everything you do, or you excel in nothing you do.

5. The Cherngs repeat: "We take seriously the concept that to lead is to serve." (Sounds like Jesus's model of servant-leadership.) "Put into action, that means helping Panda team members improve their livelihood and in the process enjoy a fuller life."

6. The Cherngs not only encourage continuing education, but also encourage team members to take care of themselves physically, mentally, spiritually, and emotionally.

The happy conclusion to all this, the Cherngs emphasize, is that "[w]hen we, the leaders and our team members, do *all* things well, it obviously means we are treating our customers well."

7. When Panda hires, they hire people who will speak up when something is not right. Panda wants committed-to-excellence team members who will not let things slip by.

8. Panda looks for people who look to the future and search for solutions.

"We look for forward-action and solution-oriented people, not any backward moaning and griping," repeat the Cherngs.

Panda's summary for business leaders:

1. Panda is about employees who grow personally and professionally.

2. Panda management exemplifies the phrase of Jesus "Where your heart is, there your treasure will be also." Panda teaches: Love your job, love your boss, love your colleagues, love the service you provide, and love your customers. Put your heart into it. *When you do what you love, people will love what you do.*

3. Panda is obviously a big fan of the application of Jesus's statement "You must be perfect as your Heavenly Father is perfect." Decades ago, Tom Peters wrote a bestseller by the title *A Passion for Excellence*, which enriched many companies and municipalities. "Yes," Panda acknowledges, "we all know that 100 percent perfection and 100 percent excellence is elusive, but pursuing excellence is attainable and sets a path toward perfection."

4. Panda puts the welfare of its employees before its own.

5. Panda emphasizes positive thinking. "Positive thinking is what we teach, express, and expect from our team members."

Positive thinking obviously works, dramatized by the fact that Panda Express is exploding in profit and visibility.

The Power of Positive Thinking

Question: So what is this "Positive Thinking" that successful business leaders embrace?

Positive thinking means faith in God and in his principles and power.

When Norman Vincent Peale wrote his classic *The Power of Positive Thinking*, the title was *The Power of Faith in God*. His publisher asked, "Who do you want to read this? Do you want the general public to read it, or do you want just the church crowd to read it? Do you want it in every bookstore, or do you want it in just Christian bookstores?"

"Well, of course," Peale said, "I want everyone to read it."

"Well, then, let's change the title. The power of faith in God *is* positive thinking," his publisher emphasized. Hence the new and successful title, *The Power of Positive Thinking*.

Wrapping it up . . .

Here, fellow business leader, is your brief and positive elevator speech, encompassing the leadership words and leadership examples of Jesus Christ:

> I respect team members, challenge them to greatness, release their energies and talents, allow them to fail, invite their comments, and reward them well. I realize that this approach to team members is the right thing to do. I also recognize that this

approach builds a company, deepens employee commitment, expands the customer base, increases customer loyalty, inspires repeat business, and—as a serendipity—enriches the bottom line, called profit.

2

Jesus on Money

2a. Don't Love It

2b. Do Give It

Part One: The Gift of Giving

Part Two: Are You a Flint, Sponge, or Honeycomb?

2c. How to Earn It

Part One: Employee

Part Two: Self-Employed

Part Three: Business Leader: The Boss

2d. How to Make It Grow: Power, Profit, Peace of Mind, and Putting People First

Part One: Jesus on Growing Money

Part Two: Jesus's Talent Parable

Part Three: Jesus's Tower Parable

Part Four: The Tower Parable and the Power of Critical Reasoning

Part Five: Jesus's Mustard Seed Parable: Let My Money Grow

Part Six: Jesus on Taxes

How to Make It Grow

Power, Profit, Peace of Mind, and Putting People First

The man with two bags of gold came. "Master,"
he said, "You entrusted me with two bags of gold.
See, I have gained two more."

The Master replied, "Well done, good and
faithful servant. You have been faithful with
a few things. I will put you in charge of many
things."

—Matthew 25:23

2

Jesus on Money

2a. Don't Love It

2b. Do Give It

Part One: The Gift of Giving

Part Two: Are You a Flint, Sponge, or Honeycomb?

2c. How to Earn It

Part One: Employee

Part Two: Self-Employed

Part Three: Business Leader: The Boss

2d. How to Make It Grow: Power, Profit, Peace of Mind, and Putting People First

Part One: Jesus on Growing Money

Part Two: Jesus's Talent Parable

Part Three: Jesus's Tower Parable

Part Four: The Tower Parable and the Power of Critical Reasoning

Part Five: Jesus's Mustard Seed Parable: Let My Money Grow

Part Six: Jesus on Taxes

How to Make It Grow

Jesus on Growing Money

Jesus and *growing money*?

My money?

Jesstaminnit!

Again, isn't this the guy . . . sorry, the God . . . who said:

1. The Son of Man has nowhere to lay his head. . .
2. Blessed are the poor . . .
3. A person's treasures are in heaven . . .
4. It is harder for a rich man to enter heaven than a camel to go through the eye of a needle . . .
5. You cannot serve God and money.

Yes, he said all that. But don't cut him short. Here's what it means:

1. "The Son of Man has nowhere to lay his head . . ."

Jesus was talking about *his* immediate task of preaching, emphasizing the urgency of *his* task. He was pointing out he had no interest in earthly pursuits like building a career or building a business. He had an eternal task to accomplish.

2. "Blessed are the poor . . . *in spirit."*

Jesus was applauding all those who have an attitude of humility, openness, and service, an attitude essential for eternal happiness, as well as earthly happiness.

3. "A person's treasures are in heaven . . ."

Heaven is a place of pure love, and a person who practices pure love is a person who's enjoying heavenly treasures now.

4. "It is harder for a rich man to enter heaven . . ."
So, who's the rich man Jesus is talking about? We talked about him earlier: he is the one who is for me,
for me,
for me.
He will never get into heaven because heaven is a place for people who are motivated by service to God and service to others.

5. "You cannot serve God and money."

Right.
Serving money, like serving sex, food, or power, is idol worship. God hates idol worship because it robs the worshipper of embracing the only loving and trustworthy object of worship, God himself. It also robs the worshipper of the joy of serving God and people.

Jesus never condemned money and riches per se. To the contrary, what Jesus did say about growing money was brilliant and practical. Two parables demonstrate Jesus's attitude about growing money.

2

Jesus on Money

2a. Don't Love It

2b. Do Give It

Part One: The Gift of Giving

Part Two: Are You a Flint, Sponge, or Honeycomb?

2c. How to Earn It

Part One: Employee

Part Two: Self-Employed

Part Three: Business Leader: The Boss

2d. How to Make It Grow: Power, Profit, Peace of Mind, and Putting People First

Part One: Jesus on Growing Money

Part Two: Jesus's Talent Parable

Part Three: Jesus's Tower Parable

Part Four: The Tower Parable and the Power of Critical Reasoning

Part Five: Jesus's Mustard Seed Parable: Let My Money Grow

Part Six: Jesus on Taxes

How to Make It Grow

Jesus's Talent Parable

A man called his servants and entrusted his wealth to them. To one he gave five bags of gold, to another two bags, and to another one bag, each according to his ability. Then he went on his journey. The man who had received five bags of gold went at once and put his money to work and gained five bags more. So also, the one with two bags of gold gained two more. But the man who had received one bag went off, dug a hole in the ground and hid his master's money.

After a long time the master of those servants returned and settled accounts with them. The man who had received five bags of gold brought the other five. "Master," he said, "you entrusted me with five bags of gold. See, I have gained five more."

His master replied, "Well done, good and faithful servant! You have been faithful with a few things; I will put you in charge of many things. Come and share your master's happiness!"

The man with two bags of gold also came. "Master," he said, "you entrusted me with two bags of gold; see, I have gained two more."

His master replied, "Well done, good and faithful servant! You have been faithful with a few things; I will put you in charge of many things. Come and share your master's happiness!"

Then the man who had received one bag of gold came. "Master," he said, "I knew that you are a hard man, harvesting where you have not sown and gathering where you have not scattered seed. So I was afraid and went out and hid your gold in the ground. See, here is what belongs to you."

His master replied, "You wicked, lazy servant! So you knew that I harvest where I have not sown and gather where I have not scattered seed? Well then, you should have put my money on deposit with the bankers, so that when I returned I would have received it back with interest.

"So take the bag of gold from him and give it to the one who has ten bags. For whoever has will be given more, and they will have an abundance. Whoever does not have, even what they have will be taken from them. And throw that worthless servant outside, into the darkness, where there will be weeping and gnashing of teeth."

—Matthew 25:14–28

In this story, Jesus applauds:

- Entrepreneurship
- Risk-taking
- Investing

Jesus on Money

2a. Don't Love It

2b. Do Give It

Part One: The Gift of Giving

Part Two: Are You a Flint, Sponge, or Honeycomb?

2c. How to Earn It

Part One: Employee

Part Two: Self-Employed

Part Three: Business Leader: The Boss

2d. How to Make It Grow: Power, Profit, Peace of Mind, and Putting People First

Part One: Jesus on Growing Money

Part Two: Jesus's Talent Parable

Part Three: Jesus's Tower Parable

Part Four: The Tower Parable and the Power of Critical Reasoning

Part Five: Jesus's Mustard Seed Parable: Let My Money Grow

Part Six: Jesus on Taxes

How to Make It Grow

Jesus's Tower Parable

Suppose one of you wants to build a tower. Won't you *first sit down and estimate the cost* to see if you have enough money to complete it? For if you lay the foundation and are not able to finish it, everyone who sees it will ridicule you, saying, "This person began to build and wasn't able to finish." (Luke 14:28–30, my emphasis)

In this story, Jesus applauds:

- The principle of planning
- Common sense
- Critical reasoning

Together, these two parables constitute Jesus's principles of stewardship and profit.

"I still don't get it. I can't picture Jesus telling us how to get rich or how to make money grow."

I know.

For centuries, millions have been imprisoned in a paradigm that says, "Jesus wants me poor" or "Poverty is a virtue" or "All rich people are crooks."

I understand. Maybe two other teachings of Jesus will help.

"Love your neighbor."

Period.

Did you get that? Love your neighbor. Period. That's it. Or is it?

No, what Jesus said was "Love your neighbor *as yourself.*"

We have a biblical, healthy, and practical obligation to take care of ourselves, to do good to ourselves, and then do the same for others. That's what love means. Love means doing good.

You know the story of the adult with the child on a plane. As the plane ascends, the flight attendant stands in front, faces the two hundred passengers, and drones with a familiar message: "If we experience turbulence and a temporary interruption of airflow, two yellow bags will drop from the ceiling above you. If you are with a child, *place the bag over your mouth first.* Then place the bag on the child."

Got it!

Got to take care of yourself so you can take care of others.

Another helpful verse: "It's more blessed to give than to _____ (you fill in the blank)." That was an easy one. "It's more blessed to give than to *receive.*"

Here's the point: "You can't give it if you ain't got it."

Charitable institutions like churches, Christian schools, colleges, rescue shelters, food banks, hospitals, and missionary outposts have been built and continue to be sustained by God's people who have accumulated wealth and given that wealth away to build his kingdom by serving people.

How do you grow your money? Are you growing it in such a way that it enriches you and your family and eventually helps many others in God's kingdom?

Let's see.

Jesus on Money

2a. Don't Love It

2b. Do Give It
Part One: The Gift of Giving
Part Two: Are You a Flint, Sponge, or Honeycomb?

2c. How to Earn It
Part One: Employee
Part Two: Self-Employed
Part Three: Business Leader: The Boss

2d. How to Make It Grow:
Power, Profit, Peace of Mind,
and Putting People First
Part One: Jesus on Growing Money
Part Two: Jesus's Talent Parable
Part Three: Jesus's Tower Parable
Part Four: The Tower Parable and the Power of Critical Reasoning
Part Five: Jesus's Mustard Seed Parable: Let My Money Grow
Part Six: Jesus on Taxes

How to Make It Grow

The Tower Parable and the Power of Critical Reasoning

During thirty years of financial counseling, I've asked people *how* they make their decisions on investments—that is, how they grow their money. I want them to think hard about how they choose strategies to make their money grow. Typical answers:

- That's what my parents always did.
- That's what my spouse wants to do; I just go along.
- I received a cold call.
- I received direct mail.
- I went to a seminar/dinner.
- I just picked what my company offers me.
- The bank or broker's office is just around the corner.
- I saw it on TV or heard it on the radio.
- I received a hot tip.
- It was convenient at the time.
- I got a referral.

None of these is prudent, rational, or profitable. None of these follows Jesus's story of the Tower Principle. Jesus's tower story urges us to plan, plan, plan.

"Estimate the cost," he said.

Esteemed neurosurgeon Dr. Ben Carson summarized the truth this way: "If I go ahead with this venture or investment, what is the *best* that can happen to me? If I go ahead, what is the *worst* that can happen to me?"[1]

If I *don't* go ahead, what is the best that could happen to me? If I *don't* go ahead, what is the worst that could happen to me?

Go ahead . . . think of a financial decision you're contemplating, and write your own responses to Dr. Carson's perceptive questions.

When I talk to clients about the best and worst in investments and financial strategies, I mean, of course, realistic expectations. In Fantasyland, the best that could happen would be an investment that doubles every day. Maybe every hour. That's fantasy.

The worst is that I could lose all my money by tomorrow. That's possible, but it usually doesn't happen that quickly.

Neither scenario is realistic. What's the best and the worst that can happen to me in light of the realistic pattern of the stock market or mutual funds, for example? The realistic pattern based upon one hundred years' history is that it may average 5 to 6 percent return per year. The worst is that it will lose 50 percent of its value in one or two years, which actually happened to millions of investors during the last two bear markets. In that case, my $500,000 will drop to $250,000. My $100,000 will drop to $50,000. My

$2,000,000 will drop to $1,000,000 in one year, and it will take ten years to recover.

The best scenario: gain 5 to 6 percent a year.

The worst scenario: lose 50 percent in one year.

So the question is this: Does the prospect of the best, 5 to 6 percent a year, outweigh the worst scenario, namely losing 50 percent in one to two years?

Normally, the answer to that is . . . it all depends. If I'm in my twenties or thirties, I may be able to recover from the 50 percent loss during the rest of my working years. But, the time I'm in my fifties and over, I probably want to avoid that worst-case scenario since I can't afford a 50 percent loss.

To examine the reality of risk, I tell clients to write a T-chart and examine the risk level of the investment or financial strategy they are considering.

This is truly the Tower Parable in action: planning way ahead. In the middle, on top, write the name of the financial strategy you're thinking about.

On the upper left, you write Disadvantages/Limitations. On the upper right, you write Advantages/Benefits.

Call it common sense. I call it *critical reasoning*, a discipline I taught in the university in my section on Introduction to Logic. Don't skip over this. And don't think you can do it in your head. It's imperative that you go through this exercise and write it down. This exercise helps you to determine (1) your personal and financial goals and (2) what strategies you are using to achieve them.

Everything we do in life that's important, we write it. When we buy a home, we write. We sign the closing

Financial Strategy: _____	
Disadvantages/Limitations	**Advantages/Benefits**

documents. When we marry, we write. We sign the marriage contract. When we buy a car, we write. We sign the car title.

Write *your* reasons for *your* investment choices and the reasons against them.

Every investor is as different as his or her fingerprints. It's important that you see what your financial fingerprints are.

Savings (Passbook savings, CDs, money market)	
Disadvantages/Limitations	**Advantages/Benefits**
Low return – 1% or less	Safety of principal.
100% taxable	In a local bank or credit union. Down the street. Convenient.
Partially liquid. CDs and some money market accounts may have restrictions.	9:00 a.m. money, available for emergencies instantly. Quick.
Not suitable for substantial monthly income, or long-term growth.	FDIC[2] guaranteed.
Subject to probate and seizure.	

Here we go. This is how *critical reasoning*, in a T-chart, applies to a savings account: The T-chart helps one to analyze any investment strategy: Stocks, Bonds, Mutual Funds, Annuities, Real Estate, Oil and Gas, Fixed Index Life Insurance, Precious Metals, Art and Antiques, Life Settlements, and others.

The purpose of this T-chart and critical reasoning analysis is not to recommend or condemn any financial strategy. Everyone has different:

- Financial goals
- Financial history
- Financial comfort level
- Income needs

- Tax obligations
- Legacy planning

A person's financial profile is as uniquely different as his or her fingerprints. No two are alike. Although I do not urge you to adopt any specific investment strategy, I do urge you to use critical analysis when making such a decision. The reason is that, after those thirty years of financial counseling, I've heard hundreds of stories like this:

- Dr. Gallagher, they didn't tell me that it wasn't liquid and that I couldn't get money out for ten years.
- Dr. Gallagher, they didn't tell me there was such a huge downside risk.
- Dr. Gallagher, they didn't tell me that the company could go bankrupt.
- Dr. Gallagher, they didn't tell me that I couldn't get monthly income.
- Dr. Gallagher, they didn't tell me how to communicate with my parents (or children) about my money and distribution plans.
- Dr. Gallagher, they didn't tell me about the possible benefits of living trusts.
- Dr. Gallagher, they didn't tell me about the Five Wishes I want my family to know.

If these investors had used *critical analysis* and asked the right questions up front, they would have understood the potential benefits and drawbacks of their investment strategies and would have been able to control the risk and substantially improve their planning. For example, the investor who wants hard assets in his portfolio is completely different from the person who wants 100 percent protection of principal. The person who wants to generate monthly income is completely different from the person who is looking to double his money every year or two. The person who invests for his legacy—children, grandchildren, favorite charity, etc.—is completely different from the person who intends to get all his money out in one year to pay off his house or buy land.

No one can make those decisions for you; it's intensely personal. It's sacred. So, using *critical analysis,* decide 1) what you really want and 2) what strategy you will use to get what you want.

Now get a plan going, as Jesus urged in his Tower Parable. Here it is again:

Suppose one of you wants to build a tower. Won't you first sit down and estimate the cost to see if you have enough money to complete it? For if you lay the foundation and are not able to finish it, everyone who sees it will ridicule you, saying, "This person began to build and wasn't able to finish." (Luke 14:28–30)

Jesus's Tower Parable: Critical Reasoning and Investment Strategies*

Stocks	
Disadvantages/Limitations	**Advantages/Benefits**
Huge possibility of loss.	Huge potential for gain.
Lack of diversity.	Liquidity.
Dividends and gains are taxable (unless in qualified accounts).	Participation in the capital markets.
Not suitable for generating monthly income.	Can enhance profit potential with: • Dividends • Stock splits • Covered calls.
Requires several for diversity.	Can build wealth passively without active management (buy-and-hold strategy).
Need a long-term timeframe.	Pride of ownership.
Subject to churning/broker abuse.[3]	
No guarantees. Highly volatile.	
Requires maintenance and oversight unless you use a professional. Then, in some cases, requires *more* maintenance and oversight.	

* Note: All investments involve risk, including possible loss of principal. Suitability is the key, and one size does not fit all. Past performance is no guarantee of future results. Always check with your tax, legal, and financial advisors before moving forward on any decision.

Bonds (Corporate)	
Disadvantages/Limitations	**Advantages/Benefits**
Can be called away. You may not be able to keep them until maturity.	Higher interest rates than a bank or a credit union usually.
100% taxable.	Possible alternative to CDs.
Requires several to enjoy diversity.	Profit potential when sold.
No guarantees regarding price depreciation or value when sold.	Could be used for predictable income (usually every 6 months).
Subject to bankruptcy and collapse.	Fixed rate of return.
Long-term time frame required for full maturity.	Could be a hedge against a bear market in equities.

Bonds (Municipal)	
Disadvantages/Limitations	**Advantages/Benefits**
Low rate of return.	Interest is tax free for current income.
Could be called away.	Measure of safety.
Dependent upon the soundness of the issuing municipality.	Generates tax-free income every six months.
May lack diversity.	May generate a net yield to the owner greater than CDs or savings.
Will generate taxes when sold because of capital gains.	Possible capital gains when sold, if sold for a profit.
Interest is not tax free when computing Social Security revenues.	

Mutual Funds	
Disadvantages/Limitations	**Advantages/Benefits**
When the trend dies, so does the fund frequently.	Participation in capital markets.
May be hard to make money since the rate of trading within many mutual funds is 75%.	Liquidity.
Potential for loss is huge.	Diversity.
Mutual funds fees are approximately 1 to 1.5% per year. The investor pays the fee whether the funds make a profit or not.	Professional management.
Relatively poor performance. 85% of fund managers normally do not meet the passive movement of the S & P 500 index.	Can be used for growth or income.
The larger the mutual fund, the smaller the profits to clients in many cases (spread too thin).	Could have diversity among stocks, bonds, real estate, and precious metals.
Phantom taxes.	Potential for huge profit.

Annuities

Definition: An annuity is an investment issued by an insurance company with guarantees provided, usually by the underlying insurance companies. In many states, there is also a provision for some type of "Insurance Guaranty Corporation," which may help to protect the investor against loss.

Four types:

- Fixed Rate Annuity
- Fixed Index Annuity (a.k.a., Fixed Index Account)
- Income Annuity (a.k.a., Immediate Annuity)
- Variable Annuity

Fixed Rate Annuity	
Disadvantages/Limitations	**Advantages/Benefits**
Relatively low rate of return compared to equity investments.	Fixed rate of return. There's a maturity date several years out with a fixed rate of return, similar to a fixed maturity date with a bank CD.
Generally a lock-in period of five to ten years.	Safety and guarantees provided by the underlying insurance or annuity company. Look for A Rated or A+ Rated.
Partial liquidity—can take out 10% per year usually, or 50% at once, depending upon the company.	Net rate return to client may be two to three times greater than that of saving accounts, CDs, or treasury bonds.
Surrender charges may apply if all the money is taken out in the early years.	No stock market risks to principal or profits.
	Lawsuit protection (in many states).
	Long-term commitment. No active management required. Sleep well at night.
	Tax deferred—same for all annuities.
	At death, proceeds go directly to a named beneficiary or beneficiaries. Same for all annuities. This bypasses probate.

To put in perspective the unique features of a Fixed Rate Annuity, let's compare it to a Bank CD*:

$100,000	
Bank CD	**Fixed Rate Annuity**
1% annually = $101,000 at year end.	3% annually = $103,000 at year end.
Subject to probate.	Not subject to probate (beneficiary provisions).
Subject to lawsuits.	Not subject to lawsuits.
Yearly gain is 100% taxable. Assume a 15% tax bracket, meaning the owner nets $850 on the $100,000 deposit, and this means that the net, net is only .85%. This is less than a 1% return.	Yearly gain is not reportable for current taxes.
Net to owner is $850 gain.	Net to owner is $3,000 gain.

* At this writing, this is an accurate comparison based upon national averages.

Fixed Index Account	
(also known as Equity Index Annuity)	
Disadvantages/Limitations	**Advantages/Benefits**
Partial liquidity—can take out 10% yearly. In some cases up to 50%, without surrender charges.	No stock market or bond market risk to principal or to the profits generated.
CAPS/Participation rates.	Average annual rate of return 5–6%.[4]
Full surrender period may be 5 to 10 years.	Passive investment (sleep well at night).
	Lawsuit protection, in many states.
	Potential for huge gains without market surprises.
	Turn into guaranteed lifetime income.
	Market is up and the investment is up. Market is down and the investment does not go down. Principal and profits are locked in.
	Tax deferred—same for all annuities.
	At death, proceeds go directly to a named beneficiary or beneficiaries. Same for all annuities. Bypasses probate.
	No stock market risk or bond market risk to principal or profit.

Some of my radio listeners and participants in the strategy known as the Fixed Index Account compare it to Matthew 7:24–27:

> "Therefore everyone who hears these words of mine and puts them into practice is like a wise man who built his house on the rock. The rain came down, the streams rose, and the winds blew and beat against that house; yet it did not fall, because it had its foundation on the rock. But everyone who hears these words of mine and does not put them into practice is like a foolish man who built his house on sand. The rain came down, the streams rose, and the winds blew and beat against that house, and it fell with a great crash."

When you build your money on a rock, you build it where principal and profits are protected. You don't allow your principal to be drowned by floods (market crashes) or your profits to be smashed by the torrent of winds (interest rate reversals).

You build on a rock. You never go backward. You go only one way: up!

Here's what it looks like:

The solid line is the stock market, including equity mutual funds and variable annuities.

Points:

1. Both accounts (solid line and dotted line) started with $100,000.

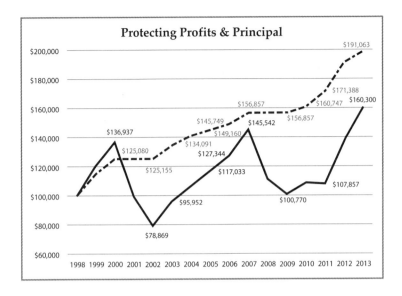

Protecting Profits & Principal

2. The $100,000 on the solid line (stock market) rocketed to $136,937 in two years. Not bad. But then, within 1.5 years, it plunged to $78,869. About a 50 percent drop. It clawed its way back up to $145,542. But then a bear market attacked again and the account fell to $100,770. A 45 percent drop. The solid line shows a typical pattern: every five years (historically), there is a bear market wiping out gains.

3. By contrast, the Fixed Index Account, the dotted line, locked in the principal and profits. It does not go backward. So when the stock market account was worth $100,770, the Fixed Index Account was worth $156,857. And when the stock market account was worth $160,300, the Fixed Index Account was $191,063.

    And the $191,063 will never go backward.

Income Annuity	
(also known as Immediate Annuity)	
Disadvantages/Limitations	**Advantages/Benefits**
No access to the principal, since the principal is used exclusively to generate monthly income.	Guaranteed income for a stated period of time, including lifetime.
Cannot change the income stream.	Predictable income not subject to interest rate changes or market fluctuations.
	Income that's largely tax sheltered.
	The schedule and amount of income stream cannot be changed. For some, this is a benefit because it can be ideal for custodial accounts for a person in need (children, elderly, retiree, trust accounts, etc.).
	Lawsuit protection.
	Not subject to Medicaid seizure.
	At death, the balance of funds remaining go directly to the named beneficiary or beneficiaries. This bypasses probate. The guaranteed income stream can also be passed on to the beneficiary (or beneficiaries).
	No stock market or bond market risk.

Variable Annuities	
Disadvantages/Limitations	**Advantages/Benefits**
Limited liquidity.	Huge potential for profit.
100% taxable as capital gains when withdrawn.	Some guarantees with some companies upon full maturity.
Vanishing product. Many companies have dropped their variable annuities programs because of complaints.	Can generate monthly income if professionally managed and kept to maturity.
Long surrender period.	Tax deferred—same for all annuities.
High fees: 2.5–3% paid by the investor whether the annuity is earning a profit or not.	May provide lawsuit protection in some states.
Subject to stock market or bond market risk.	At death, proceeds go directly to a named beneficiary. This bypasses probate.
	Diversity of investment choices within the annuity.

Real Estate

With the publication of Robert Allen's, Donald Trump's, and Robert Kiyosaki's books and tapes, the opportunity to be a direct investor in rental homes and real estate projects has become very attractive and very popular. This chart will help you in *your* analysis of real estate opportunities.

Real Estate (Residential/Single Home Rentals or Apartment Rentals)	
Disadvantages/Limitations	**Advantages/Benefits**
Periodic onsite inspection.	Predictable cash flow, i.e., as long as the rent continues to come in.
Danger of depreciation on the house, need for a new roof, etc.	Appreciation in the value of the house or property.
One bad renter can wipe out years' worth of profits.	Many tax benefits, including depreciation, possible corporate write-offs, etc.
Need to be a jack-of-all-trades or be able to hire somebody at low prices to do the electrical, AC, plumbing, etc.	Pride of ownership.
Owner needs to live in the neighborhood, or in the proximity, for periodic oversight.	Not subject to stock market cycles.
	Diversity in a portfolio.

Oil and Gas	
Disadvantages/Limitations	Advantages/Benefits
Speculative.	Huge tax write-offs.
May require drilling time.	Potentially attractive cash flow.
Infrequency of checks and the amount of return.	Diversity.
	Direct participation in capital expansion.

Fixed Index Life Insurance (Universal Life)	
Disadvantages/Limitations	Advantages/Benefits
High cost of premiums (compared to term insurance).	Provides the usual benefits of life insurance characterized by the phrase, "Is your life worth a D.I.M.E.?" (see below).
Limited liquidity.	Tax-free growth/income.
High maintenance fees.	Allows for larger contributions than IRAs. Can be used for private pension plan.
May take years to build cash value.	Open ended.
	Partial liquidity.
	May provide substantial tax-free income at retirement.
	Not subject to lawsuits or seizures in most states.

Proceeds from life insurance provide, to the beneficiaries, these standard benefits:

Debt liquidation

Income for life

Mortgage payoff

Education expenses for children or grandchildren.

All tax free.

How to Multiply Your "Dime"

Life insurance now has substantial *Living* Benefits, as well as the traditional Death Benefits (i.e., those proceeds to the beneficiaries).

Let's say that the Death Benefit is $300,000.00. With today's enhanced life insurance, you don't have to wait until you die to get the money. You can access money from the Death Benefit now . . . yes . . . while you are still living.

This is a powerful benefit for unexpected medical bills, or other family emergencies. Not suitable for all, but check it out.

Precious Metals (Gold, Silver)	
Disadvantages/Limitations	**Advantages/Benefits**
Limited liquidity.	Alternative to equity-type accounts for growth. Possible alternative to bank-type accounts for safety.
No guarantees. May be as volatile as stocks or bonds.	Appreciation potential.
Metal held is subject to theft or loss.	Diversity.
Storage fees may apply.	An investment you can "hold in your hand."
	Pride of ownership.
	A hedge against inflation.
	Nostalgic value (historic coins).

Art and Antiques	
Disadvantages/Limitations	**Advantages/Benefits**
Illiquid.	Diversity.
No possibility of current income.	Profit potential.
Possibility of loss from theft or fire.	Nostalgic or historic value.
High cost of insurance possibility.	Family treasure.
	Potential for tax write-off.

Life Settlements (The Compassion Strategy)	
Disadvantages/Limitations	**Advantages/Benefits**
Not liquid. Not designed for current income.	Potential to provide double-digit returns.
Possible uncertainty of life expectancies.	Passive investment (sleep well at night).
Premium calls may be applied at some point.	No active management required.
	No taxes paid while growing.
	Provides benefit to needy and appreciative people, i.e., people who sell their unwanted policies to raise case for urgent needs.
	Potential to control gains in the future.
	No stock market risk.

There are other investment strategies, which I have not described here:

- Commercial real estate
- Debt-buying programs
- Tax liens
- Multi-level marketing
- Venture capital projects

. . . and many more.

The fourteen I've examined—and you have analyzed with me—are the most common and those on which I've received the most questions in my thirty years on the radio, in the classroom, at client appointments, and through media appearances.

Bottom Line

Does a *critical reasoning* chart, in examining the risks and rewards of investments, work? Ask the captain:

"Dr. Gallagher, I retired as a pilot nearly thirty-five years ago. I had $650,000 then. I rolled it over with some guy in a brokerage firm. I told him all that I needed was $1,000 a month. OK, it was my fault. I didn't check my statements. I kept thinking $1,000 was going to my bank account. I noticed the principal was going down, but I thought that was just the stock market's normal cycle. And then when I really started looking at my statements, it was worth $425,000. I was still taking out $1,000 a month.

"I didn't know any better, so I transferred to another broker in another brokerage firm, and I still didn't write down what my plans were. Like the first guy, he told me I just needed a lot of the right stocks and some good mutual funds. What I didn't realize at the time was good growth meant good growth for him.

"The cycle of getting ripped off happened two more times before I finally ended up with just $45,000, and I still need to get that thousand dollars a month."

So how do we help this ninety-year-old pilot nearly in poverty? $45,000 left, and he still needs at least $1,000 a month.

As I pointed out earlier, our mission statement at the Gallagher Financial Group includes the commitment to help people, whatever their need is. So . . . through a variety of creative resources and support services both within our company and without, we've been able to keep this pilot afloat, or maybe in his case, in the air; still, it's tragic that he ended up, like millions of investors do, on the ash heap of poverty after forty years of productive work.

He sent me a card later. "Just wish I had met you and your company twenty-five years ago. I would still have my $650,000. Wish we had gotten together sooner."

By not using critical reasoning, my pilot friend overlooked the fact that the stock market is not a place to protect your principal and have predictable lifetime income—which were his specific needs. If he had written down the advantages and disadvantages of the stock market and looked at them clearly, he would have realized in the beginning that the stock market was not suitable for his long-term retirement goals. Not only would he have realized this, but it would have protected him from being abused later on by unscrupulous brokers.

Does *critical reasoning* work in examining risks and rewards? Ask another captain.

Dear Dr. Gallagher,

Nelson and I would like to take this time to thank you and your staff for allowing us to retire "safe, happy, and early."

We began our journey toward retirement planning around ten years ago. We met with several financial advisors, letting them know what our retirement goals were. We let them know that we wanted immediate help with managing our 401K and 403b accounts and guiding us through our journey toward retirement.

When visiting the local library, we saw an advertisement regarding your upcoming visit to discuss financial planning and retirement. We received a copy of your book, *The Money Doctor's Guide to Taking Care of Yourself When No One Else Will*. You were very approachable and kind enough to sign our book.

When we arrived, we received a very warm welcome. Thus began our first steps toward understanding what our retirement would look like. With each visit, we were treated with the utmost regard. Our questions were always answered to ensure understanding. We laughed, we worked, and we began to feel safe and secure. We began to understand that a safe retirement was possible for us.

As the economy began to tumble and American Airlines rumors began to surface rapidly, Nelson paid a visit to the AA company retirement office. With a clear understanding of what he needed to retire safe and happy, he was able to confidently retire earlier than he had originally planned. He began his retirement on August 1st, taking a lump sum from American Airlines.

When American Airlines announced that they were filing for bankruptcy, we absolutely couldn't believe it. Nelson always felt that this was a possibility, but thought it was a year or more away. We said a prayer of thanksgiving. Our friends called us and asked if Nelson had a crystal ball at home. We immediately said, "Yes, the Gallagher Group."

We cannot thank each of you enough for your help and understanding. God truly blessed us with each of you. Thank you all, from the bottom of our hearts.

With much love and appreciation,
Nelson and Cindy

Putting It Together

In addition to his Tower Parable, which taught investors how to plan, Jesus also taught how to select a planner, whether his title is CFP, CPA, stock broker, insurance agent, mutual fund salesman, or financial planner.

This is the question you ask him or her: "If I didn't have any money with you, would you still care about me?"

In this world there is a wide, thick line. Above the line are people, and below the line are things. God has made us to love people and to use things. You want to find out immediately if the financial advisor you are sitting with cares about you *as a person* or looks at you as an object of profit. So when you ask that question you will see an instant response.

Most, unfortunately, will not know how to answer. If the financial planner stammers and looks at you like a deer in headlights, or says, "That's a dumb question," or laughs nervously and tries to divert the question, then that is a sign to grab your briefcase and run from the office. You must know, up front, that your financial planner looks upon you as a person of unconditional worth and not merely as an object of profit.

God has directed, and Jesus emphasizes, that things are to be used and people are to be loved. Jesus said: "What good is it for someone to gain the whole world, yet forfeit their soul?" (Mark 8:36).

In Jesus's perspective, persons are to be intrinsically valued one at a time: "In the same way, I tell you, there is rejoicing in the presence of the angels of God over one sinner who repents" (Luke 15:10).

God unconditionally loves people—one at a time. And that is the kind of love and respect you want from a financial planner. You must understand, in the investment world, cash is *not* king. Character is king. *You* understand this principle.

But does the financial planner understand it?

Stephen Covey said it right. You either practice integrity in everything, or you practice integrity in nothing.

Is your financial planner building her practice slow and steady? Or is she looking for quick riches? Is she personally handling money God's way? Is she generous in a spirit of giving? Does she see her profession as a higher calling? Does she have a record of church, community, or charitable service? Is it clear that she loves what she does, following the dictum "If you do what you love, people will love what you do"? Does she see financial planning as a ministry of service?

Does she understand that *people are primary*?

Take this quiz:

1. Name the five wealthiest people in the world.
2. Name the last five Heisman trophy winners.
3. Name the last five winners of the Miss America contest.
4. Name ten people who have won the Nobel or Pulitzer Prize.
5. Name the last half dozen Academy Award winners for best actor/actress.

Now let's see how you do on Quiz B:

1. List a few teachers who aided your journey through school.
2. Name three friends who have helped you through a difficult time.
3. Name five people who have taught you something worthwhile.
4. Think of a few people who have made you feel appreciated and special.
5. Think of five people with whom you enjoy spending time.[5]

You stumbled on Quiz A. And you scored big on Quiz B. We rarely remember famous people. We always remember people who cared.

People are more important than profits, and relationships are more important than revenue. That's the fundamental truth Jesus Christ showed us by his words and by his work.

Notes

1. Dr. Ben Carson is the author/hero of *Gifted Hands, Think Big, Take the Risk,* and *America the Beautiful: Rediscovering What Made This Nation Great.*

2. FDIC = Federal Deposit <u>Insurance</u> Corporation. Yes, Insurance covers bank deposits as well as insurance and annuity deposits.

3. See Arthur Levitt's book *Take on the Street: What Wall Street and Corporate America Do Not Want You To Know* (Pantheon, 2002).

4. Jack Marrion, *Index Annuities: Power and Protection* (St. Louis: Advantage Compendium, 2004).

5. Dennis Fakes, *G.R.A.C.E: The Essence of Spirituality (iUniverse,* 2001), 146.

Jesus on Money

How to Make It Grow

Jesus's Mustard Seed Parable: Let My Money Grow

A popular strategy for tax deferral in non-qualified accounts is the annuity.[1] It's like Jesus's story of the mustard seed:

> He told them another parable: The kingdom of heaven is like a mustard seed, which a man took and planted in his field. Though it is the smallest of all seeds, yet when it grows, it is the largest of garden plants and becomes a tree, so that the birds come and perch in its branches. (Matt. 13:31–32)

The mustard plant starts off small, just like the two-dollar illustration given below, and it grows into the largest in the garden.

But what if the mustard seed, as it blossomed into a bush (later a tree) . . . what if its branches were attacked and chopped each month? It would not be the largest in the garden that Jesus talked about.

Ditto with your money. What if it was attacked and chopped?

The Story of the Dynamic Dollar

The question is sometimes asked:

"What good is tax deferral? You're going to have to belly-up to Uncle Sam sooner or later."

Excellent point.

Remember, you'll give to Caesar *only* what is Caesar's. You'll pay taxes, but that doesn't mean you have to pay every month of every year for the rest of your life.

Just for illustration—

Let's suppose you have two bucks and that two bucks will double *every month.*

What do you think you'll have at the end of twenty months? (Remember, it's just two bucks.)

Answers range from $180,000 to $650,000.

How about this? $1,048,576!

Your account rocketed to $1,048,576 because you *deferred* taxes.

Check it out:

Double 1	$2.00
Double 2	$4.00
Double 3	$8.00
Double 4	$16.00
Double 5	$32.00
Double 6	$64.00
Double 7	$128.00
Double 8	$256.00
Double 9	$512.00
Double 10	$1,024.00
Double 11	$2,048.00
Double 12	$4,096.00
Double 13	$8,192.00
Double 14	$16,384.00
Double 15	$32,768.00
Double 16	$65,536.00
Double 17	$131,072.00
Double 18	$262,144.00
Double 19	$524,288.00
Double 20	$1,048,576.00

Now let's suppose you did NOT defer taxes. You paid taxes as you went along.

Here's what it looks like:

Double 1 less 25% of the gain =	$1.75
Double 2 less 25% of the gain =	$3.06
Double 3 less 25% of the gain =	$5.36
Double 4 less 25% of the gain =	$9.38
Double 5 less 25% of the gain =	$15.41
Double 6 less 25% of the gain =	$28.72
Double 7 less 25% of the gain =	$50.27
Double 8 less 25% of the gain =	$87.96
Double 9 less 25% of the gain =	$153.94
Double 10 less 25% of the gain =	$269.39
Double 11 less 25% of the gain =	$471.43
Double 12 less 25% of the gain =	$825.01
Double 13 less 25% of the gain =	$1,443.76
Double 14 less 25% of the gain =	$2,526.58
Double 15 less 25% of the gain =	$4,421.51
Double 16 less 25% of the gain =	$7,737.64
Double 17 less 25% of the gain =	$13,540.88
Double 18 less 25% of the gain =	$23,696.54
Double 19 less 25% of the gain =	$41,468.94
Double 20 less 25% of the gain =	$72,570.64

Question: Would you rather end up with $72,570.64 or $1,048,576?

"Hold on, Dr. Gallagher," I hear you say. "On that $1,048,576 . . . the guy has to pay taxes at some point!"

Right.

Here's what it looks like.

The average American household is in the 32 percent tax bracket. We'll be conservative and assume only 25 percent bracket.

So, after paying taxes he is left with $786,432.00.

I'll revise the question. Would you rather have $72,570.64 or $786,432.00?

Notes

1.   Annuities can also be used in qualified accounts.

Jesus on Money

How to Make It Grow

Jesus on Taxes

In two places, Jesus addressed the issue of taxes:

> "But so that we may not cause offense, go to the lake and throw out your line. Take the first fish you catch; open its mouth and you will find a four-drachma coin. Take it and give it to them for my tax and yours." (Matt. 17:27)
>
> "Then Jesus said to them, 'Give back to Caesar what is Caesar's and to God what is God's.'" (Mark 12:17)

Jesus respected the reality of taxes and, like Americans today, he didn't appear to be enthusiastic about this; but get real. They're here.

Here's what I would add to this statement: "Give back to Caesar *only* what is Caesar's."

Don't pay any more in taxes than you have to.

You can find much better uses for your money than giving it to the government. Right?

Four tax control strategies:

1. Tax free
2. Tax efficient
3. Tax credits
4. Tax deferred

Tax Free

Municipal bonds are tax free. You own municipal bonds as individual bonds, or in a tax-free bond fund. (Caution: *not* tax free when added in with your Social Security income.)

Another tax-free strategy is the Roth IRA. You put $3,000 a year into your Roth IRA. You do that for twenty years. That's $60,000. Let's say it compounded and grew to $200,000; it is all tax free. Forever

- Tax free to you
- Tax free to your spouse
- Tax free to your kids
- Tax free to your grandkids
- Tax free to your favorite charity.

And it's *not* slapped onto your Social Security income.

Look seriously at the potential benefits to you of a Roth IRA.

Tax Efficient

A fund that is 5 percent more tax efficient potentially increases its returns nearly 10 percent.

A fund that is 10 percent more tax efficient potentially increases its return nearly 20 percent.

How do funds do this? Understand, first . . .

1. Funds that hold dividend-paying stocks get whacked with taxes. Dividends are taxable and scream, "Tax me! Tax me! Tax me!" on your 1099.

2a. Funds that buy/sell, buy/sell, buy/sell get whacked with taxes. A "buy/sell" strategy bangs out capital gains. Capital gains are taxable and show up on your 1099.

    Managers of tax-efficient funds avoid the strategies described above; they avoid holding dividend-paying stocks and avoid using "buy/sell" strategies.

    These managers generally hold two hundred to five hundred different stocks and let the stocks appreciate passively. They buy XYZ stock at $10 and let it grow . . . to $15 to $20 to $30. They do not sell the XYZ stock. They do not generate capital gains. They do not hold dividend-paying stocks, since the payment of dividends would potentially generate a taxable event.

    This tax-efficient fund with XYZ stock and hundreds of other stocks rises just like a shallow pond at seaside rises. When the tide rushes in, the shallow pond, every drop of it, rises.

2b. Another tax-efficient strategy is to own *individual stocks* . . . not stocks in a mutual fund.

You buy two hundred shares of ABC company at $10 a share. Cost $2,000. Shoots to $15. You hold. Shoots to $25. You hold. Shoots to $50. You hold. Wow, your $2,000 is now worth $10,000. You made $8,000. And no taxes on it. Why? No sale. With individual stocks, you decide when to sell and when to get hit with taxes.

What if I need the $8,000 now? Get a loan. Pay a little interest, and avoid the 20 percent in taxes.

Tax Credits

Tax credits are for folks who are mad, really mad, about paying taxes. They will do anything legal to cut taxes. They like tax credits.

There are three profit potentials on tax credit programs:

Profit 1: A long time ago, Uncle Sam said they wanted more retirement housing for seniors. They went to private real estate companies and said, "You build them, you get the investors, and we'll give you a tax break." The companies said, "Sold." For every $5,000 you invest in one of these programs, you get an approximately $700 tax credit. So, at the end of the year, you figure up your taxes. You owe the IRS $2,300. You say, "Whoa, I remember I have a tax credit of $700." $2,300 − $700 = $1,600. So, you know that check you just wrote to the IRS for $2,300? Tear up that check, and write a new one for $1,600. That is an immediate savings of $700. That is money in your pocket.

It gets better. For the one-time investment of $5,000, you get this $700 tax credit every year for ten years. At the end of ten years, you put in your pocket $7,000 total tax credits. For your initial investment of $5,000, you get $7,000 back. Put in $50,000. You get $70,000 back every ten years.

Profit 2: Since you are an owner of a senior citizen retirement village, you get to write off depreciation on your yearly taxes. Your CPA will show you how to do this. You can write off depreciation expenses year after year.

Profit 3: At the end of the ten-year program, that's when the properties are split and you get a split of the profits.

When you put together the three different ways to profit, you potentially can realize an average return of 10 to 13 percent.

Tax Deferred

The most popular tax-deferred strategies: 401Ks, 403Bs, 457s, Keoghs, SEPs (Simplified Employee Pension plans), and IRAs. The most popular is the 401K. Three ways you potentially make money with your 401K:

1. The 401K contributions are not added to your taxable income. If you make $50,000 a year and put $5,000 into your 401K, that $5,000 is working for you. You own it. However, as far as the IRS is concerned, you received only $45,000 in taxable income, because $5,000 is considered to be a pre-tax contribution.

2. Money grows on a tax-deferred basis. You put in $5,000 a year. Let's say you put it in a good fund and you earn

(on average) 10 percent a year. Over 20 years, you put in $100,000 in tax-deferred money. It grows to $399,852. Still tax deferred. As you take money out for income, you will be paying normal taxes from a larger nest egg because you allowed it to grow on a tax-deferred basis.

3. Many companies offer a company match. For every dollar you put in (up to 6 percent), the company will put in $0.50. That means for every dollar you put in you have an immediate gain of 50 percent.

Note: The 401K lump-sum amount that you are accumulating is *your* money. In many cases, you can "roll it over" to an account or strategy of your own choosing. Even if you are still working for the company.

This positive action of "rolling over" your 401K could potentially add safety, liquidity, and profitability to your account.

3

The Bountiful
Attitudes

You've examined your heart and your perspective toward money, acknowledged that we are all financial flops, and recognized that your resources have been entrusted to you—not to be loved or loathed but to be leveraged. As a faithful steward, you know that you are expected to earn money with courage and integrity, spend it wisely, and grow it with care and foresight.

What comes next? Where do you go from here?

As you move forward, grabbing your goals with intention and purpose, seek to employ what I like to call the Bountiful Attitudes. These eight truths, commonly called the Beatitudes and stretching from Matthew 5:3 to Matthew 5:12, speak to the kingdom of God in the hearts of men and women. They showcase godly attitudes and eternal rewards. And they are intensely relevant when applied to the urgent issues of money and success.

Be very clear what the word *blessing* means. Each verse begins with it: blessed are the poor in spirit, blessed are the pure in heart, blessed are those who are peacemakers, etc.

Blessed simply means a high-five from God.

When you're pure in heart (for example, Beatitude number 6), God praises you. To be blessed by God means he applauds your actions and attitudes. He is jumping up and down in the heavenly bleachers and giving you the wave. He is high-fiving you from heaven.

Don't get it at first?

That's OK. His audience didn't get it, either.

Everything Jesus said in the Beatitudes shattered the Pharisees' idea of holiness. Everything Jesus said in the Beatitudes shattered the Romans' idea of power. Everything Jesus said in the Beatitudes shattered earthly ideas about wealth.

Then and now.

The eight Beatitudes *do* apply to worldly wealth, as well as heavenly riches. That is why I call them the *Bountiful Attitudes*.

Bountiful Attitude One

Blessed are the poor in spirit for theirs is the kingdom of heaven. (Matt. 5:3)
This is the spirit of being humble, receptive, and teachable. Willing to learn from God and others and open to ideas for progress and improvement. God honors the poor in spirit and showers blessings upon them.

Look at Solomon: "Give thy servant an understanding of how I may discern between good and evil" (1 Kings 2:9).

The next verse says: ". . . and this request pleased the Lord."

Because of his humble receptivity to God's leading, he became one of the world's wealthiest men and the leader of a nation.

Bountiful Attitude Two

Blessed are those that mourn, for they shall be comforted. (Matt. 5:4)

Comforted by whom? Comforted by God. This refers to the stark realization that every man and woman comes to eventually: *It's time—way past time—to turn to God for comfort and rescue and solutions.* Like the hymn says, "Where could I go but to the Lord?"

This verse is coupled with Romans 8:28: "And we know that in all things God works for the good of those who love him, who have been called according to his purpose."

And, this is further coupled with Jesus's statement: "I have overcome the world" (John 16:33).

Many people deny themselves the blessings of this bountiful attitude because they feel it's a sign of weakness to look to God for comfort and strength. Just the opposite— it's a sign of common sense to say, "I need help." When you say, "I need help," it's like you are sitting in a theater, and the curtain rises on a huge stage. Suddenly, you can see all the glorious dancers, singers, and actors in front of you, and a world of possibilities appears for getting the comfort and solutions that you need.

Bountiful Attitude Three

Blessed are the meek, for they shall inherit the earth. (Matt. 5:5)

Unlike the popular notion of meekness being equated with weakness, meek is *not* weak. Only two people in the Bible were called meek, Moses and Jesus. Meek means being quietly and firmly positive. Meek means strength under control. It takes a strong man or woman to forgive one's own financial hurts or financial betrayals by others. When they do, they will inherit the earth.

"Meek" means not to take anything personally. You're stronger than that. You deny yourself the cowardly collapse of reminiscing on previous hurts or failures, either by you or by others.

You are meek—you have strength under control—just like Moses and Jesus.

Bountiful Attitude Four

Blessed are they that hunger and thirst after righteousness for they shall be filled. (Matt. 5:6)

What did hunger and thirst really mean when Jesus said it? Then, food was scarce and water was precious. Christians have a hunger to use money wisely. Christians thirst for the pleasure of righteous living and righteous giving.

Money is neither good nor bad any more than a car is good or bad. A car can be used to rush a sick person to the hospital. A car can also be used to kill. You find out real quick when it comes to investing that cash is not king, *character* is king. A righteous attitude toward money is powerful and fundamental.

Bountiful Attitude Five

Blessed are the merciful, for they shall claim mercy. (Matt. 5:7)

Listen to others!

The greatest need a person has is to be listened to . . . understood . . . accepted . . . unconditionally loved. This is mercy with skin and sweat on it. Millions are crippled by guilt and fear. They are ashamed that they lacked financial discipline. They *painfully* regret their impulsive decisions with investments, and they fear the consequences. They need a friend or financial counselor who will be merciful and understanding, no matter what mistakes a person has made. And, of course, this is followed up by prayerfully exploring solutions with this person burdened by guilt, fear, and shame.

Bountiful Attitude Six

Blessed are the pure in heart, for they shall see God. (Matt. 5:8)

The pure in heart see the best. They see the best in themselves, and they see the best in others. They see the best in adversity, knowing that with God's power they will turn adversity into opportunity. The pure in heart are always looking for ways to use money to help other people and to glorify God.

The pure in heart have a fixed goal. They want their lives to be used by God in the powerful use of skills and money. The pure in heart understand this truth: My life is not a series of jobs and careers to gather money. My life is a mission, a passion to serve others. This is purity of purpose; this is purity of heart.

Bountiful Attitude Seven

Blessed are the peacemakers, for they shall be called the sons of God. (Matt. 5:9)
The peacemaker seeks peace of mind for himself or herself and for other people. It's more than an absence of strife. It's having a plan for yourself and for others that brings harmony and blessings. When you're at peace with yourself about your money and you help others have a sense of peace about their money, that attracts the favor of God.

Bountiful Attitude Eight

Blessed are those that have been persecuted because of righteousness, for theirs is the kingdom of heaven. Blessed are you when people insult you, persecute you, and falsely say all kinds of evil against you because of me. Rejoice and be glad, because great is your reward in heaven. (Matt. 5:10–12)
The joyful person does not collapse under criticism or pressure. When you have a bountiful attitude, you will at times attract people who are jealous, resentful, and deceptive. "In fact, everyone who wants to live a godly life in Christ Jesus will be persecuted . . ." (2 Tim. 3:12).

Hold fast to your faith and your integrity even when you are under attack. It is wholly worth it. When you employ the bountiful attitudes in your life, you will find yourself enjoying the benefits of a grateful heart and an eternal perspective. Where you acknowledge the Creator of all wealth, the blessings will follow. You will find that your love-inspired, Christ-centered life adventure is like a pencil.

The Parable of the Pencil

A pencil, you say?

Consider:

- A pencil points in any direction you hold it. Keep it pointed toward your goal (remember the one you wrote on your card?), and carry your goal with you. This is the card you keep posted on your bathroom mirror, dashboard, refrigerator, and above your computer.

- Keep the point sharp. You don't saw a tree with a blunt saw. You sharpen the saw. Sharpen your skills. Keep reading, listening, growing, learning. Progress comes with busting paradigms and smashing through comfort levels.

- Your pencil, your life, is powerless without someone to guide it. Your passion for your goal is the *force* to guide it. Ask God to guide you. God loves to help people fulfill their people-serving, life-enhancing goals.

- The pencil needs pressure to apply lead to paper. The pressure you apply is your passion to share with people your goods and services, your gifts and talents, whatever they may be, and build a profit for yourself.

- A pencil can write many things:

  — A thank-you note to your third grade teacher or first boss
  — A love note to your mate
  — An encouraging note to children or grandchildren
  — A thank-you note to parents
  — A note of appreciation to employees or coworkers
  — A letter of acceptance for your new position

  A pencil can also write:

  — A suicide note
  — A terrorist threat
  — A letter of resignation
  — A hate letter to an ex-spouse

The pencil is pointless without a purpose. That purpose can be positive and progressive, or hateful and destructive. Depends on how you direct your pencil, how you direct your life.

- Your pencil has an eraser. You make a mistake, you erase it, and keep writing. Forgive yourself and move on. "But . . . I've already written it. I sent it out. I can't erase it."

Yes, you can.

Call. Write. Visit. Correct. Apologize.

Start over.

"But what if I can't 'start over'?"

Maybe the proposed recipient of the apology is dead or the mistake is absolutely irreversible.

That's where regret, fatigue, and discouragement always attack. You find yourself saying, "I wish I could start over." "I should have done this." "I should have done that."

Shove the "shouldas" in the "john" and flush them. Remember, *what you've got now and where you are is plenty good enough to build again.* Yard by yard anything seems hard, but inch by inch, anything is a cinch. Start over and shout it loud: "I will bring something good out of my mistakes and failures."

You have had failures, but you are not a failure.

- The pencil breaks. So what? Take the half that's left, sharpen it, and keep writing.

When you keep writing, keep planning, and keep working toward your purpose-charged goal, you earn the title CS—Courageous Steward.

So . . . go back now, and sign your card with your sharp pencil. With your new title, CS. Go ahead. Do it now.

Martin Burns, CS, or

Andrea Powers, CS

As a Courageous Steward, you have your own GPS as well:

Goals + **P**lan = **S**uccess.

That's your divinely-inspired and sure-to-succeed *GPS*.

When you write your plan and follow your plan for responsible stewardship and profit, you will have peace of mind and profitable experiences. And, eventually, you'll be able to teach God's plan for profit to others, including those who may at one time have been your fierce opponents.

Rejoice for the opportunity God has given you. Your reward is in heaven even as you experience some of that heavenly joy now.

Bonus

What Is the "Bite" in Your Financial Plan?

You want to examine every investment for its possible "BITE":

B = exposure to BEAR MARKETS.

I = exposure to INFLATION.

T = exposure to TAXES.

E = exposure to EXPENSES.

Stocks

Bear Market—Are stocks subject to a bear market? Absolutely:

- 93 percent loss in 1929.
- 25 percent loss in one day, October 19, 1987.
- 50 to 60 percent loss between 2001 and 2002.
- 45 percent loss in 2008.

These numbers are not merely academic.

Let's say a retired couple had a $500,000 portfolio of stocks in 2000, from which they were drawing $2,500 a month. When the bear market hit them, they found their nest egg sliced in half. Now they've got only $250,000.

They've got two choices. They can continue to take out $2,500 a month and see their original deposit melt rapidly, or they can cut their income and reduce their food, travel, grandchildren's gifts, medical expenses, etc.

A widow who had $500,000 in stocks found that within eight months in 2008, she had only $300,000. Again, she could either cut her income or severely cut her lifestyle.

For many, the reality hits hard: "I've got to go back to work," "I can't afford to help my grandchildren with college," or "I can't afford the medical devices that my spouse needs."

Tough decisions. Brutal decisions. Painful decisions.

All because someone didn't use critical reasoning to plan, plan, plan.

Inflation—Are stocks subject to inflation risk? Potentially, no, providing the stock is profitable. (Just the opposite. Stocks are frequently touted as being a strategy that can beat inflation.)

Taxes—Are stocks subject to taxes? Yes.

Expenses—Are stocks subject to expenses? Yes. Commissions in, commissions out, and/or management fees.

Corporate Bonds

Bear Market—Are corporate bonds subject to a bear market? Absolutely. Bonds go up, and bonds go down.

Inflation—Are bonds subject to inflation? No, normally bonds are a good hedge against inflation.

Taxes—Are corporate bonds subject to taxes? Yes.

Expenses—Are corporate bonds subject to expenses? Yes. Costs money to buy them, costs money to sell them, and they may incur management fees.

Municipal Bonds

Bear Market—Are municipal bonds subject to a bear market? Yes.

Inflation—Are municipal bonds a good hedge against inflation? Normally, yes.

Taxes—Are municipal bonds subject to taxes? No, except in the case of Social Security taxes and capital gains when municipal bonds are sold.

Expenses—Are municipal bonds subject to expenses? Yes. Costs money to buy them, costs money to sell them. May also incur management fees.

Mutual Funds

Bear Market—Are mutual funds subject to a bear market? Absolutely. In the crises of 2001 and 2008, mutual funds went down an average of 40 percent.

Inflation—Are mutual funds a good hedge against inflation? Potentially, yes.

Taxes—Are mutual funds subject to taxes? Yes, *even if the mutual fund goes down in value.* In that case, they are subject to phantom taxes. Investors pay for reinvested dividends and capital gains even if they are not profitable.

Expenses—Are mutual funds subject to expenses? Commissions coming in, commissions coming out, and annual management fees up to 1.5 percent.

Fixed Annuities

Bear Market—Are fixed annuities subject to a bear market? No.

Inflation—Are fixed annuities a good hedge against inflation? Probably not. At this writing, a fixed annuity maybe will pay 3 percent. Better than a CD, but still 3 percent. (Inflation is running at 4 percent.)

Taxes—Are fixed annuities subject to taxes? No.

Expenses—Are fixed annuities subject to expenses? Yes, in the form of surrender charges if a person cashes in early, although a person normally can take out 10 percent a year without surrender charges, or have the surrender charges waived in certain circumstances. No monthly fee.

Fixed Index Accounts

Bear Market—Are fixed index accounts subject to a bear market? No, because when the market goes up, they go up, but when the market goes down, they do not go down.

Inflation—Are fixed index accounts a good hedge against inflation? Yes, because they can enjoy the profits of the general stock market without stock market risk.

Taxes—Are fixed index accounts subject to taxes? No.

Expenses—Are fixed index accounts subject to expenses? They may have caps or participation rates, and there may be charges for early surrender.

Overall, the fixed index account may potentially come the closest to protecting your money against the BITE of the strategies we've looked at.

Income Annuities (Immediate Annuities)

Bear Market—Are immediate annuities subject to a bear market? No.

Inflation—Are immediate annuities subject to inflation? Depends upon the rate of return you were promised from the annuity company. If the rate of return is high enough, say 7 to 9 percent, that could definitely resist inflationary pressure.

Taxes—Are immediate annuities subject to taxes? Partially.

Expenses—Are immediate annuities subject to expenses? No.

Variable Annuities

Bear Market—Are variable annuities subject to a bear market? Yes. When the market goes down, the variable annuity goes down. That's why it's called a variable annuity.

Inflation—Are variable annuities a hedge against inflation? Potentially, yes, just like stocks or mutual funds.

Taxes—Are variable annuities subject to taxes? No, not during the accumulation period, but when sold, they can generate huge capital gains.

Expenses—Are variable annuities subject to expenses? Yes. The average is 2 percent a year. Whether the value of the variable annuity is up or down, investors are still paying the money manager, insurance company, or brokerage firm 2 percent a year, or more.

Real Estate

Bear Market—Is real estate subject to a bear market? Yes, a bear market in land values or home values.

Inflation—Is real estate a hedge against inflation? Yes.

Taxes—Is real estate subject to taxes? Yes, capital gains when sold; however, there are other tax-advantaged strategies associated with real estate.

Expenses—Is real estate subject to expenses? Yes, anytime you buy, anytime you sell a property, and, of course, insurance and property upkeep. Important to make sure that the net return to the real estate investor exceeds all the potential expenses, including repairs, insurance, and taxes.

Oil and Gas

Bear Market—Is oil and gas subject to a bear market? Yes, a bear market in petroleum products.

Inflation—Is oil and gas a hedge against inflation? Traditionally, yes.

Taxes—Is oil and gas subject to taxes? Partially. (Tax write-offs along with cash flow can help offset income taxes.)

Expenses—Is oil and gas subject to expenses? Sometimes, the owner/operator will require more money for more drilling or production costs.

Precious Metals

Bear Market—Are precious metals subject to a bear market? Yes, when there are fluctuations in the precious metals market.

Inflation—Are precious metals a hedge against inflation? Traditionally and historically, yes.

Taxes—Are precious metals subject to taxes? Yes, when sold.

Expenses—Are precious metals subject to expenses? Normally, no, unless there is a need for storage fees or if held in a brokerage account.

Art and Antiques

Bear Market—Are art and antiques subject to a bear market? Yes.

Inflation—Are art and antiques a hedge against inflation? Potentially, yes.

Taxes—Are art and antiques subject to taxes? Yes, when sold.

Expenses—Are art and antiques subject to expenses? Normally, no, other than possible storage or security expenses.

Life Settlements

Bear Market—Are Life Settlements a hedge against a bear market? Yes.

Inflation—Are Life Settlements a hedge against inflation? Yes.

Taxes—Are Life Settlements subject to taxes? Yes, at the point of redemption.

Expenses—Do Life Settlements have ongoing expenses? Normally, no. Exception in cases where life expectancies go beyond normal estimates.

As stated in our initial disclaimer:

> Every investment involves some type of risk.
> Every investment has a *"bite."*

So. . . It is not enough to say, "I'll just buy a good mutual fund and sit on it."

Or, an oil well,
Or, a piece of land,
Or, a bag of gold or silver,
And just sit on it.

Do you know what you're sitting on? Could your strategy collapse? Could your strategy support you for a lifetime of income?

I urge you to use the principles in this book to find out and make the necessary adjustments.

These are Jesus's principles for a worry-free financial future, and to him be the glory.

Your financial friend,
W. Neil Gallagher, PhD

About the Author

W. Neil Gallagher, PhD, is a financial journalist, investment counselor, and seasoned broadcaster. As the host of *Family and Financial Fitness*, Dr. Gallagher has fielded thousands of questions related to financial communication, estate planning, wealth creation, family enrichment, and the psychology of investing. Author of *The Money Doctor's Guide to Taking Care of Yourself When No One Else Will*, Dr. Gallagher is the financial speaker for Zig Ziglar's *Born to Win* seminars and a member of Kingdom Advisors. Having conducted hundreds of programs for employees and retirees of several Fortune 500 companies,

Dr. Gallagher maintains a private practice of individual and institutional clients totaling $1 billion.

Dr. Gallagher earned a doctorate from Brown University and is the author of five books and seventy popular and scholarly articles featured in publications including the *Journal of Value Inquiry*, *Charisma/Christian Life*, *World Vision*, *Bottom Line* magazine, and *The New American*.

Dr. Gallagher is a former stockbroker with a major Wall Street brokerage firm and, later, a St. Louis brokerage firm.

To arrange for a speaking appointment with Dr. Gallagher or for media interviews, please call 800-434-4362 or e-mail neil@gallagherfg.com.

Jesus Christ, Money Master is accompanied by a leader guide and a student guide. These are profitable, inspirational, and effective resources for congregational, classroom, or small-group study. To place your order, please visit www.NeilGallagherBooks.com.